ROAD JUICE

Live, Eat, Drive, Dream, and Get Better At It

PATRICK CAFONE

ISBN: 979-8-89316-887-7 (paperback)
ISBN: 979-8-89316-886-0 (ebook)

Attention: this is not your practice life; this is really your life!

We all make many little choices every day. Life is all about choices. Some people are easygoing and happy, while others are intolerant and sad. Some live lonely lives, while others have tons of friends and a vibrant social life. Some have love in their lives, others do not. Many people eat healthy meals while others feed on all kinds of junk. Certain people are very comfortable behind the wheel, while others struggle while at it. The list can go on and on for pages!

What are the reasons for these differences? All of the contrasting scenarios above are the end result of the many small decisions we've made over time. As the saying goes, you can't do the same things over and over again and expect to get different results. It's insane to even think of it, but I guess we are all insane sometimes.

I always loved the saying, "Everyone wants to change the world, but no one wants to change themselves." One thing is for sure: you are going to get old someday, and the last thing you want to happen is for you to look back and say to yourself, "I wish I did this or that when I was younger." This ain't no practice life. You only have one life to live, so you need to go for it all while you're alive. Follow your dream and choose to do the things that will make you happy, both now and in the future.

Are you normal? What is normal? Normal is just a cycle on a washing machine! Life moves around in a cycle, like a washing machine. Whatever you do at this phase spins round and comes back to you with its repercussions later in life.

If you notice a pattern you are stuck in that may not be beneficial in the future, it's in your best interest to effect a change now. But before you can do that, you have to care—and unfortunately, many people don't care. The truth is, change takes a little work, and it's way easier to just stay in that rut. Let's admit it: we are all kind of lazy!

But wait—change can be fun! It's good stuff, and changing for the better is what life's all about. I believe in you! I think you can change—yes, even change your beliefs. It's just a decision, and you make little decisions every day!

When you wake up in the morning and look in that mirror, there are a couple things you need to realize. First of all, you are unique! There is no other human with your DNA. There is something you can do better than anyone else can. You're on this earth for a reason. Repeat this out loud: "There is a reason why I am on this earth! There is something I can do better than anyone else, and I can share that information to make the world a better place!"

Having this mindset alone fires up your spirit. It can change your life—big time—and bring you everything you ever wanted from this world.

One of the most beautiful things about life is that you have the power to decide how it all turns out. Your thoughts and mindset shape your story. It's up to you to decide, because inside your head is *your* town. When you received it, it was blank. From the moment you grew into a conscious being, you've been writing the story of your life. And even right now, you're still scribbling in that book. You have the freedom to write whatever you want. You can write it to be the greatest story ever told.

Not everyone shares this sentiment. Some say, "What goes around comes around." Others say, "It is what it is." John Lennon said, "Instant karma's gonna get ya," and yet others say, "It's destiny; you have no control over what happens."

That's horseshit.

I believe you have more control than you realize over what unfolds in your life. A famous motivational speaker called Charlie "Tremendous" Jones once said, "Our lives basically change in two ways; the people we meet and the books we read." When you read, you travel—so why travel to the same places? Here's a chance to make some changes! Have some *Road Juice;* it's a life additive. Don't just have a boring, day-to-day life; wake up and live an amazing one!

First concept: you have to be a believer. You have to believe that only you can control what you think about. You have to realize that every human has the capacity to have a good attitude, no matter the circumstances. I am hammering on this for a reason. This is an important reality. Every human has the capacity to have a good attitude, no matter the circumstance.

What is Road Juice? The "road" is a path you follow on a journey. In this case, we are talking about the "road" of life. "Juice" is the essence of something. So, "Road Juice" provides some guidance that will help in the journey of your life.

I have carefully studied many facets of life and squeezed out this juice for you, so you can more easily make your life more meaningful. My goal is to give you the push you need to tweak your brain and hit your refresh button. Then you will learn how to live, earn, love, drive, eat, and have an exciting, loving, happy, wonderful, and creative life!

There are no chapters in Road Juice; there are only exits. Just like in the United States, odd-numbered highways go north and south (I 95) and even-numbered highways go east and west (I 90). In Road Juice, odd numbered exits are about life, even numbered exits are about driving, and exits with letters (exit 1 A) are about eating and drinking.

Have a great trip!

You may ask yourself, why would I want to read *Road Juice*?
Here are a few possible reasons:

- It's entertaining.
- You could learn to eat "better"
- You will have a healthier, happier life.
- To find tips for living longer.
- To be safer on the roads.
- To have a good laugh.
- It will make your life "easier"
- You will get back to basics, as in, KISS (Keep It Simple, Stupid).

- You will learn how to "RTFD" (Read the Freakin' Directions).
- To remember to listen to some good tunes you haven't heard in a while!

Which influential people have shaped your life, and why? What are the influential events that have shaped your life, and why?

We humans yearn for a better life. This is why it's important to receive input from admirable sources and tweak our lives for the better in whatever endeavor we've chosen to pursue. *Road Juice* follows the concept of "tweaking our lives for the better." The keys to life are learning, growing, and making a positive addition every day.

I have heard so many great sayings over the years—here are a few of my favorites: "Give a man a fish, feed him for a day; teach a man to fish, feed him for life," and, "Your mind is like a parachute, it only works when it's open," and, "It is not the strongest or the most intelligent that survives; it is the one who can adapt to change."

Life is a learning experience. Sometimes, you have to keep an open mind and be willing to look at things differently in order to learn. Key statement: "look at things differently." Some people can pull the string on that chute quite easily; others can't. Why are some people rigid and others flexible to new ideas? I think it's an "ego" thing; some people think they "know it all," whereas others are searching for knowledge. I bring it up in a couple of exits again, but here's the question: are you a done deal, or a work in progress? If you answered, "work in progress," pull the string on that chute and enjoy the ride! Don't forget, a parachute typically saves your life, and once you open that parachute, it stays open (watch out for it getting tangled). Go ahead, free fall for a while then pull the string on that chute! Enjoy the view and the trip.

When you read, you travel to many wonderful places and learn from others' experiences. Never give up on learning, and keep an open mind to new ideas. Learning makes our lives better! You can achieve anything in life, if you are willing to give up whatever you must give up to achieve your goal. If we did not learn, we would still be living in caves, rubbing two sticks together to make a fire for heat and cooking. As humans, we have come very far—especially in the last twenty years, with the internet and the digital era. You can get any information you wish with the swipe of a finger. You are constantly learning. We went from taking those first few simple steps when you were an infant, to now driving, changing lanes, doing eighty mph, drinking coffee, looking at a report, communicating on the phone, and asking Siri for answers! Yes, we sure have learned a lot.

The world is changing faster than you think. It is so fast-paced that everyone is in a hurry! Because of that, we have learned to have very bad eating habits. We have learned to take antidepressants. Every time we don't feel good, we pop a freakin' pill! We have learned to take energy drinks, to sit in our car and wait in the drive through rather than walking inside for a product. We should have enough time to make some of these products at home, but we are in too much of a hurry.

We have learned that because of the leveling out of the world economies, both husbands and wives have to work. Children are now brought up by strangers in daycare centers, and we have forgotten the importance of sharing family meals together. The most advertised products on TV are for erectile dysfunction or vaginal dryness.

And—one of my favorites—we have learned that you have to have four-wheel drive to be safe when you are driving in the rain.

YES, THE WORLD HAS GONE CRAZY!

Yes, life is getting more complicated. Everyone is multitasking and in a hurry because they want to get things done fast, and move on to something else. What a drag that we all want to be somewhere else. When I look around, I see people sitting next to each other and instead of talking, they text each other. It is a wild and crazy world!

All that being said, every day, ideally, we keep learning, tweaking our mindset, and putting new ideas into practice. Every day, we must fight off all the crazy negative stuff and keep trying to believe that the world will get better. Our daily lives involve constant thinking, so you may as well think positive and think big!

Where have we learned all these wonderful skills of driving, talking to Siri, and eating in the front seat of our cars? Is it from our upbringing and people we have encountered? Or is it from deep in our genes? The ongoing question for centuries: is it nature or nurture? I'm from the school of thought that it's more "nurture." We all learn from every little experience that we encounter in our lives, starting with our parents, siblings, relatives, teachers, friends, acquaintances, and even random encounters we have daily with strangers.

Well now you are encountering *Road Juice*. You can learn some interesting ideas if you will let yourself. It's a journey, and every exit has its unique scenery. Stop now and then and enjoy the "views."

You can't just go wherever the wind blows you—if you did that, who knows where you might end up? The answer is in how you set your sails. In order to set your sails, you have to know how, and you have to realize that you, and only you, are in control of setting them! I can help you learn how to set your sails with your brain. With proper settings, you can even sail *into* the wind. It's like the Capital One advertisement asks, "What's in your wallet?" The *Road Juice* commercial asks, "What's in your brain?"

There are so many decisions you have to make. You may start to wonder, what is the correct protocol for this life? The truth is, it's all about tweaking your life for the better, in all the little things you do on a daily basis. Life comprises a series of small habits—how about creating some better ones? Everything starts small, with a dream. For instance, I am following my dream of writing and publishing *Road Juice.* I have been taking notes longhand in spiral notebooks for many years, before I recently went digital.

Here are some quick concepts for when it comes to following a dream and figuring out your protocol for life: be strong; don't hang around with "clock suckers" (negative people who steal your time); "Never Give Up" trying to make the world a better place; never give up on trying to make your life better; and be careful who you spend most of your time with, because they say "you" are the sum of the five people you hang around with the most.

Why do you get up in the morning? What runs through your brain when you go to sleep or first wake up? Interesting questions—think about them. Guess what? Your dreams, or what you think about, determine your future. Never give up on your dreams, NEVER GIVE UP!

I am, by no means, some kind of life guru, but I do have quite a few ideas to share. *Road Juice* is a bunch of ideas that will help you tweak your brain toward a better life. Everyone thinks of changing the world, but no one thinks of changing themselves. Want to make a change? Try this: don't complain about anything for a week! Hello, this is a serious, life-changing challenge for you. Write down the time and date, put it in your wallet or purse, and don't complain about *anything* for a week! You will find that it is very hard to do!

Meanwhile, YouTube some of these tunes. They will take you somewhere. Start with the song "Somewhere." by Barbara Streisand. Some might think it's corny, but give it a shot. Good stuff!

EXIT 1

LEARNING TO WALK WAS NATURE; LEARNING TO CONTROL YOUR BRAIN IS NURTURE

Why do some people fill their brains with good thoughts, and others fill theirs with bad thoughts?

Training.

Some people don't realize that it is a choice. We all have the ability to choose what we think about—so why spend your time worrying about stupid stuff that probably is not even going to happen? It's simpler than you think; it's just a decision. Decide to be happy rather than unconsciously giving in to stress.

I work on it every day. When negative thoughts come into my mind, my mind starts churning away, and I have to remember Rule #1: "No projecting of negativity out into the future." Sometimes I think we are "programmed" to worry. Maybe thousands of years ago, when we were cavemen, we were always worried about where we were going to get our next meal, or how to protect ourselves from the bears, lions, or whatever. You know, worrying about the basics—food, shelter, etc. Nowadays, people are worried mostly about "bullshit." By "bullshit" I mean people are worried about stuff that never even happens, or has nothing to do with reality. To deal with this, always remember: "no projecting of negativity out into the future."

Obviously, there are a few exceptions. For instance, if you are scheduled for your annual physical next week, and you still smoke, it's natural to worry about the results of your lung X-ray. But then, why worry when you can just take action and quit smoking? You shouldn't worry about anything that you have some control over. Instead, take action, get motivated, and do something positive. Even if it's a small step, at least it's a step. To walk a mile, you have to start with a first step.

You also shouldn't waste time or energy worrying about things that are out of your control. For instance, you shouldn't worry about what other people decide to worry about. Consciously decide not to think about it. Decide today to be happy. It's so much fun to celebrate, so stop what you are doing and celebrate something great about your life right now! If you are in good health, that is something you should definitely be celebrating.

A couple studies have shown that the most important thing you can do for your health is smile. When you smile, your glands release some healthy hormones that help you live longer (the same goes for laughing). Also when someone sees you smile, their body releases hormones that help them!

According to the britishcouncil.org website, happiness produces endorphins in the brain, which transmit signals to your facial muscles to trigger a smile. This is the start of a positive feedback loop, because when our smiling muscles contract, they fire a signal back to the brain, stimulating our reward system, further increasing our level of happy hormones (endorphins). In short, when our brain feels happy, we smile. When we smile, our brain feels happier.

Fake it till you make it! If you want to be happy, just smile. If that sounds hard, no worries, just be around someone who smiles. Smiling is contagious.

When negative thoughts come into your mind, block them out and decide to think about something good. Make believe your mind is a TV—you have the remote in your hands. When negative thoughts creep in, pick up your imaginary remote control, point it at your brain, and change to the happy channel! Don't forget, remote controls are finicky little devices—you might have to point and click a couple times to get it working. Meanwhile, have you checked the batteries in your remote?

An acquaintance of mine reminded me last week that you should always try to make everyone's life less stressful, because when you do, you make your own life less stressful! People spend quite a bit of time going to the gym, exercising, and trying to eat right, but what about your brain? I believe you need to work on that even more than your physical body. Spend some time today working on your attitude, and remember—your health, happiness, friendship, and love are the most important things in life. People like to be around happy people. So, starting today, smile more and laugh at yourself a little. Put some bounce in your step. Always try to make everyone else's life less stressful, because when you do, you make your own life less stressful.

Remember what John Lennon said, *"All you need is love"* On another note, when was the last time you sang Van Morrison or Rod Stewart's song, *"Have I told you lately that I love you"* to someone? Forget about all the bullshit and love someone today. It's what makes the world go round.

Memories of Exit 1

- Only you can control your brain.
- No projecting of negativity into the future.
- You can "make believe" anything you want.
- What's in your brain?

EXIT 1A

WHICH HAS MORE WATER?

These lettered exits in *Road Juice* contain great ideas to help you get a little healthier and creative with your eating habits. Please don't only *read* these recipes; try them, and have some fun. You have choices concerning what foods you put in your body. Don't be a victim of getting stuck in the same stupid eating habits.

It is advisable to eat food with a good amount of water. Should I eat a donut or an apple? Which has more water? Always pick the food with more water, because we all could benefit by getting more water in our diet.

Secondly, always consider the color of your food! Try to eat all the colors every day ! Eat some blue (blueberries), yellow (yellow peppers and bananas), green (spinach, broccoli, Swiss chard), reds (tomatoes, raspberries, cranberries), orange (orange peppers, carrots, peaches, oranges), and white (perhaps cauliflower). Don't forget to also eat some brown (dates, coconuts). The more colors you eat, the more vitamins and minerals you get.

Be careful of the amount of fruit juice you drink. Read the ingredients. Many have tons of high fructose corn syrup. They make you think that they are very good for you, but they are loaded with sugar calories.

Watch your bread intake as well. Typically, the second or third ingredient in store-bought bread is also high fructose corn syrup. Yikes! Remember: water, vegetables, fruits, and fiber are your best bets. I hate to admit it, but I am a bread lover. What I have learned is that when you buy bread, try to buy the brand that has the fewest ingredients—typically, unbleached flour, water, and salt.

Want to live longer? Eat more plants! I learned this from the book *Blue Zones* by Dan Buettner. If you really want to have your mind blown about your food choices, read that book—or, watch the documentary called *Food Choices*.

A couple years ago, I was reading a magazine while waiting in the doctor's office when I came across an article talking about "GBOMS." It stands for "greens, beans, onions, mushrooms, and seeds." (When you think of seeds, also think of nuts). These are better than a diet of processed meat, as in baloney.

Stop buying processed food wrapped in plastic, especially cardboard boxes with plastic-wrapped, microwavable garbage. All that stuff has too many chemicals. Instead, eat more fruits, veggies, nuts, and fiber.

If you Google the healthiest foods and click on just about any site, the list is pretty much the same. This list is from drfuhrman.com:

- Green leafy vegetables (spinach, kale, Swiss chard)
- Non-leafy cruciferous (broccoli, cauliflower, cabbage)

- Mushrooms
- Onions
- Nuts
- Seeds
- Tomatoes
- Pomegranates
- Sweet potatoes
- Peppers

If you Google most unhealthy foods, here's the list you'll find:

- Sweetened dairy (ice cream)
- Trans fats (margarine, commercially prepared baked goods)
- Donuts
- Processed meat (sausage, hot dogs, lunch meat)
- Smoked meat (barbequed, well done, and charred)
- Fried foods (French fries)
- Soda
- Refined white sugar
- Refined white flour
- The poison syrup, a.k.a. high fructose corn syrup

These are very interesting lists we all could learn from. Let's get one thing straight: I am not a vegetarian, but I do try to limit my "processed meats" intake. I eat bad stuff also, but the key is in moderation! Right now, it's March, a couple days after Easter. It's eleven at night, and I just ate a couple slices of leftover Easter ham with some sharp cheddar, chopped jalapeños, and a Miller Lite. I am a bad boy sometimes. Miller Lite is kind of like water, right?

On a better note, My wonderful wife of 47 years, Deborah, made a delicious split pea soup with what was left of the Easter ham. It looks like I'm having a couple exquisite bowls of pea soup for the next few days! Peas are a type of beans, and they are loaded with water. When I re-read this Exit, it makes me think about the song "And It Stoned Me" by Van Morrison. Why not have a tall, cool glass of water right now and listen to that song?

Memories of EXIT 1A

- Drink more water.
- Read the ingredients and stop eating foods with high fructose corn syrup.
- Watch those carbs, eat more GBOMS, and eat less processed food.

EXIT 2

TAKE A BREAK FROM YOUR BRAKES

An automobile is a "freedom machine" used to get from place to place. It gives you the freedom to enjoy traveling and see places you've never seen before. A Chevrolet commercial, when I was a kid, had the slogan: "See the USA in your Chevrolet." An automobile means *freedom*.

People are bound to make mistakes while driving. While it annoys you, odds are you have made the same ones before, so chill out and be nice! First major rule of driving: keep your freakin' *ego* out of it! Who taught you to drive? Was it your father, mother, sibling, or a friend? Were they a good and highly experienced driver? Everyone considers themselves a great driver, as long as they passed their driving test. *This* is an ego thing. Despite everyone seeing themselves as an excellent driver, there are still so many road accidents, causing deaths and injuries. The body shops where they fix cars after accidents make a lot of money. It's a multi-billion dollar industry. I pay $1800 a year just for insurance!

Over ninety percent of all automobile accidents are caused by driver error. Talk about the risks of computer-controlled cars all you want—presently, humans are still responsible for controlling automobiles in a safe manner. If you Google causes of death in the United States, car accidents are consistently in the top ten. A bad decision behind the wheel can kill you, but the average person thinks they are a great driver and is not interested in learning more. To encourage you to read on, I will show you how you can save tons of money by driving correctly. You will also save a lot of energy, wear and tear, and make the world greener.

First tip: use the brakes half as much as you do now. It's quite simple to do—all you have to do is look a little further ahead to "get the big picture." Give yourself a tad more space, and don't react automatically. Instead of hitting the brakes automatically, put your foot right above the brake pedal, but don't touch it. This maneuver is called a "brake cover." If you really have to hit your brakes, you are ready–but a big percentage of the time, you never really have to use them. Avoiding the brakes saves you energy.

I have been driving for close to sixty years, sometimes over five hundred miles a day. When you drive that much, you see a lot of strange things on the road. I used to drive my girlfriend's 1952 Willys pickup. Her parents had a farm in the top northwest corner of New Jersey. I made the authorities believe I worked there, so I could obtain my "farmer's license" in 1966, when I was 16 years old. It was a different era back then. The drinking age in New York, where I went to high school, was eighteen. Everyday after class, the whole high school went drinking somewhere. Bars did not care how old you were back then.

It was also the "drag racing" era. Life was so simple that you could buy a 1957 Chevy with a V8 engine for a couple hundred bucks. Fast cars and alcohol don't mix, so many of my friends died because of drunk driving. I used to buy and sell cars to make money. I met some older guys that knew how to work on foreign cars, so I ended up flipping MGs, Austin Healey, Triumph TR3s, and VW bugs. I could smoke any of those jacked-up, front end, drag-racer guys on a country road with my Austin Healey. Back in that era, you had to learn how to drive—or you were dead.

I remember some of my drunk buddies in a GTO pushing me in a VW bug down Old Mine Road at 70 or 80 mph. I was just driving calmly, minding my business, when they pulled up behind me. Within a twinkle of an eye, they started pushing me into curves faster than a VW bug could get through. It was a scary experience, but I was already used to taking risks while driving, so I knew quite a bit about car control.

Car control is simple, if you educate yourself to feel it. Tweak the wheel to the left, and you feel your body wanting to go right. Tweak the wheel to the right and you feel your body wanting to go left. Driving simply involves hurling a bunch of weight down the road on four little rubber connections—but to drive well, you have to learn how to control all that weight! Steer where you want to go. That day was indeed scary, and I am lucky to be alive. This is why I still celebrate life everyday.

I have driven at least two million miles. I spent the better part of my life building houses (many a hundred miles from where I lived). From 2008 to 2017, I drove a gasoline tanker, tractor trailer (fifty-three tons) in a 200-mile radius of Albany, NY, in the Catskills and the Adirondacks. From 2017 to the present, I am back in the construction and remodeling business. What a long, strange trip it's been. And much of that time, I've been behind the wheel.

I often wonder, is there a driving gene? It seems some people understand time, movement, and space better than others. Most drivers seem to know how to use the brake pedal way better than they know how to use the steering wheel or the gas pedal! I think most drivers think their brake pedal is their "savior." Yes, in a dangerous situation, the brakes slow you down and can save you—but using the brake pedal wastes energy, big time. I'll bet the average driver could save a couple hundred a year on energy costs and brake wear by just understanding "space" a little better.

In everyday life, when you are talking to someone, you don't speak to them standing one foot from their face. Typically, you respect their space and stay two or three feet from their face. The same rules apply to driving. Why do people drive so close to other people, when it is not necessary? I understand if you are trying to get out of Manhattan on the Lincoln Tunnel approach ramps—obviously, to keep your position, you would have to drive very close to the vehicle in front of you. But in most everyday driving situations, there is no need to get so close to other vehicles. The person you just passed will catch up with you at the next light.

I commute forty miles each way, to and from work on a daily basis. When I hop on the interstate at five in the morning and accelerate out, there's not much traffic. The average speed of everyone varies greatly on any given day. Sometimes everyone's doing eighty-five, other days, sixty-five. But one thing's for certain: as I catch a "rat pack" (three or more cars traveling together), I wonder, why are these cars driving so close to each other? It's a wide-open road, but every thousand feet there are numerous cars traveling within forty feet of one another. Why do people do this? I believe it is because when people are driving, they are doing everything by habit, just like a herd of cows going back to the barn.

I find them amusing, but I also know that they are dangerous. That's why I drive alone, and as far away from other cars as possible. It's safer that way, and—being that I'm not near anyone—I never have to use the brakes. If I ever get close to the *cows going back to the barn,* I don't hit the brakes. Instead, I check my mirrors, signal the drivers behind me, and use the steering wheel to go around the pack. You would not believe the amount of people I see using their brakes on an empty interstate. It's a strange phenomenon, but people are "brake happy."

As I get closer to Albany and it gets more "chunktified," I check up a little bit (get off the gas) and keep a little extra distance between myself and the vehicle in front of me. At this point, I am trying to not be too close to them. I am checking my mirrors constantly so I know who is around me already—in case something wacky happens, I want to make sure I have a way out. I am conscious of the speed of the cars ahead, and I am aware of the person's personal space. I am trying not to drive them nuts by following too closely, annoying them with headlight glare.

Think about the speed of the vehicles around you. Look ahead and try to envision what is going to shake down. What's the sense of keeping your foot on the gas, realizing you are approaching someone too fast, and then have to hit the brakes? Why not check up a couple seconds earlier?

Brakes are a big waste of energy—when you use the brakes, you are just turning this energy into heat and wearing your brake pads or shoes. An object in motion tends to stay in motion, so when stopping at a traffic light, don't stop if you don't have to. Go very slow the last twenty or thirty feet, so you are increasing your odds of possibly not having to stop at all!

Here's a bit of trivia about all of the above: I have a habit of looking at the front wheel rims of cars. You can always tell how much a person uses their brakes on any given vehicle by how much "brake dust" or dirt is on the front rims of a vehicle. I live in an area where there are a lot of interstates, so there is not as much brake use as in an urban area. Often when I see front rims heavily covered in brake dust, I look at the license plate and—sure enough, it's from Jersey, where they use a lot more brakes than up here! In the future, stop being in such a hurry. Listen to "I'm In a Hurry And Don't Know Why" by the band Alabama.

Memories of Exit 2

- Keep your ego out of driving. Remember, it's OK to be nice.
- Create a new habit by using a brake "cover" instead of really hitting the brakes.
- Don't drive like cows going back to the barn; think about what you are doing.
- Check your mirrors more often and give yourself a little more space.
- When you think you have to stop in traffic, save fuel by going slower the last twenty or thirty feet instead of stopping.

EXIT 2A

SOME CHOLESTEROL

Here's the first recipe of *Road Juice!* Take a stick of butter out of the fridge and leave it on the counter for a couple of hours. When it softens, put it in a bowl. Take three or four cloves of fresh garlic, peel, and either chop finely or crush with your garlic press. Mix it up with the butter. Now, take five or ten sprigs of fresh parsley or the herb of your choice, chop them up, and put that in the mixture. Mix thoroughly and put it back in the fridge! Now, this is your new go-to butter at dinner time. You can dab a little of it on anything you're grilling in the oven, or use it to cook anything.

Throw some Italian bread slices in the toaster or broiler. Add this butter and garnish with a few tablespoons of grated cheese (Parmigiano-Reggiano is my favorite) and fresh herbs of your choice. Toast it up.

I know some people would say butter contains too much cholesterol. Well, that's true, but you can tone it down by adding some garlic, some fresh herbs, and mixing it with olive oil. The only thing is, if you use the olive oil version, I have heard that you must use it all in a day or two because the garlic can possibly grow bacteria in the olive oil mixture. I use a little of each now and then. Sad to say, the butter version is pretty tasty!

If you are still concerned about too much cholesterol, here's a remedy from the old days to cut it: mix a tablespoon of apple cider vinegar, a squeeze of fresh lemon juice, and a teaspoon of honey to a quarter glass of water. Drink it in the morning! It's an old-time farmer drink. You could also drink more red wine while you listen and dance to Bob Marley's song "Red Red Wine."

Memories of Exit 2A: Make some garlic butter! Add some herbs. If you are worried about cholesterol, use olive oil instead of butter.

EXIT 3

"THE ANSWER, MY FRIEND, IS BLOWIN' IN THE WIND"

Bob Dylan

Life is fun. Look around you and you'll see how fun it is to be alive, no matter where you live. No matter what you're going through, choose to have fun, my friend! You see these words, "my friend?" Learn to use them more when interacting with people. If you are a man, start using the word "brother" more often. If you are a woman, start using the word "sister" regularly. Greet people with excitement and a warm smile.

As Crosby, Stills and Nash sang in the song "Wooden Ships", always remember that every word means something different to every individual—but if you smile at me, I will understand, because everyone everywhere smiles in the same language.

Did you know that, deep down in everyone's psyche, there is a serious need for love and acceptance? Why not spread positivity by making people feel loved and accepted? Greeting people with a warm smile and calling them "friend" could go a long way in making them feel good.

Speaking of being positive, one of the basic rules of life is to wish everyone a happy life devoid of fear. No walking around holding grudges or wishing evil on anyone. Let go of any anger. Anger causes stress to compound. It can spike up your blood pressure, and end up killing you—killing *you,* not the person you wish evil upon. Don't be so judgmental. Learn to forgive, then forget. That is the way it works—but in order to forget, you first have to forgive. If you find yourself always judging and staying mad at people, maybe you should change your goals and reassess your priorities.

Nobody died and left you to be the "judge," so why are you so judgmental? Learn to let go. Learn to overlook, and stop caring too damn much. I have a funny sign in my garage that says, "If at first you don't succeed at something, and you are upset, try drinking a beer and see how much less you care!" Seriously, most of the things you are so upset about today won't matter in the next year. I think there are electrical connections in our brains that have built up over a long period of time, which make it easier for our brain to think negatively. I believe you have to build and reinforce new positive electrical connections to counter the effects of the negative. You need to work on strengthening these new connections by using them constantly, until thinking positive thoughts becomes your lifestyle.

One of the most sensible ways of staying positive is to be thankful. One of my older brothers who passed away thirteen years ago used to always say, "There is only one true handicap in life, and it is a bad attitude." My mom, who passed away at ninety-seven a few years ago, used to say, "Attitude and gratitude are the two most important things in life."

Here is an exercise that will help you: when you wake up in the morning and get out of bed, say "thank you" as you take your first few steps. Be thankful for the ability to walk. Yes, you have to show gratitude for even the things you take for granted. Another great tip for staying positive is to keep a list of ten thoughts that make you happy. You can write it and shove in your wallet, or just type it on your phone. When life gets you down, take a look at the list.

When I talk to someone, and they tell me how bad life is for them, I always ask them to read *National Geographic.* Somewhere in the world today, there are women walking several miles every morning to get their family their daily water. After that, they'd still have to pick up twigs to start a fire to cook a meal. If you have a roof over your head, food in the fridge, central heat, running water, and your health, then you are doing pretty good.

Life has its ups and downs; some days you're the windshield, other days you're the bug. Remember, it's not what happens to you in life that matters; it's how you deal with what happens to you. You think you have nothing to be thankful for? Close your eyes for thirty seconds and imagine being blind. Now open them and look around. Now *that's* a reason to be thankful.

We were all put on this earth for a reason. It's now up to you to find that reason and prioritize it. Maybe your purpose is to spread happiness. We are all in the same boat, and the world is a better place when we are all spreading happiness and good vibes. When you spread happiness and positivity, it becomes quite difficult for people to find faults in you.

To round up this exit, I need you to check out the song "Good Vibrations" by The Beach Boys. Also listen to "The Future's so Bright, I Gotta Wear Shades" by Timbuk 3.

Memories of Exit 3

- Smile more.
- Let go of any anger.
- Don't worry, be happy.
- Wag more, bark less.
- Try to slow things down a bit and be a more patient, generous, and loving person.

EXIT 3A

YIELD TO BREAKING BREAD

Let's break some bread. It's a shame that when many people eat, they do it hurriedly. Eating and drinking is an act of providing nourishment to your body and soul. It's something you should do peacefully, joyfully, and thankfully. It's not something you should rush through. Instead, you should normalize taking your time and allowing your body to enjoy the process.

It is way more fun to "break some bread" with other people than to do it alone. Share a meal with someone you love today. Even though George Thorogood's song says "I drink alone," I believe every meal and drink time is a time for sharing life.

Let me use my life as an example. My wife, Deborah, and I love to eat and drink. Over the years, we have cultivated a lifestyle of preparing and eating delicious meals with family and friends.

We have been together for over fifty years and we have three wonderful daughters. When the kids were younger, my wife made sure we all sat together to have dinner every night. Being that the apple doesn't fall far from the tree, our daughters have now carried on that tradition in their homes. Deborah and I invite people over for drinks and dinner quite often. Going out to a fancy restaurant is fun and relaxing, but it is expensive, so we've chosen to make our meals at home and just have fun.

"You are what you eat." We have all heard this so many times, but how many of us have paused to think about it? How many have mulled over it and asked even funny questions like "Does that mean some of these people walking around are made out of Diet Pepsi, Danishes with Styrofoam cheese, microwaved pasta, or McDonald's hamburgers?" Well, in a way, yes. If you've been eating unhealthy meals, you'll end up becoming an unhealthy person. And if you eat healthy meals, you'll live a healthy life. That's an added benefit of cooking at home.

It's fun and very nourishing to prepare your own food instead of buying factory-prepared garbage. I know you're busy, but it's all a question of priorities and time. Apart from its health benefits, you'll also save loads of money.

A few days ago, our local food store had a sale. Things were so cheap—when you bought a three- or four-pound roast, you got a free two-pound bag of carrots, a free two-pound bag of onions, and a free five-pound bag of potatoes. Let's imagine you get a deal like that. All you have to do is bring out your slow cooker, chop up all the veggies, add a little beef stock, a splash of red wine, a splash of soy sauce, and a few squeezes of double strength tomato paste. Add four or five chopped cloves of garlic, a few sliced stalks of celery, and some salt and pepper. Turn the slow cooker on, and cook. After six to eight hours, pour some glasses of wine, warm up the Italian bread, and enjoy!

After making this meal, we had so many leftovers that we cooked up a few more veggies the next day in beef stock, invited friends over, and had another wonderful dinner. All these meals cost between $15 to $20 to prepare. If you are pressed for time, the slow cooker meal is the way to go. Just chop and mix your ingredients, turn it on low heat for six to eight hours, and have a beautiful meal later.

People eating unhealthy foods always blame it on not having enough time to make a proper meal. Bad diet is one of the most common causes of the deteriorating health of the average American. Our diets have changed slowly over the last twenty to thirty years as we have gotten busier and lazier, but there are a couple simple things you can do to make it better.

Here are a few pointers:

a) Spend more time in the produce aisle when you go food shopping.
b) Eat more plants and drink more water. Water is so essential—our bodies are made up of 60 percent water.

If you don't already have the habit of drinking water, start today. Some 30 to 40 years ago, no one drank bottled water. Back then, we didn't have as many obese people as we do today. Now, bottled water is big business and many people are battling weight problems. It doesn't make any sense, but the reasons are quite simple. First off, everyone is in way more of a hurry than they used to be many years ago. Secondly, we are eating more and more processed foods, and thirdly, we no longer move our bodies as much. We have all become too lazy.

I read that when we consume processed food, our body fails to recognize such complex compounds and chemicals, so it stores them as fat. As the GoodRx.com website says, never eat or drink anything with the word "DIET" on it. It is poison to the body.

Studies have shown that artificial sweeteners like aspartame, sucralose, and saccharin may be connected to:

- Increased appetite, hunger, and sugar cravings
- Weight gain
- Blood sugar problems
- Gut microbiome problems
- Stroke
- Heart disease
- Metabolic problems

Meanwhile, a good portion of what we eat is packaged in plastic, so we end up eating a lot of plastic microparticles when we microwave these foods. Due to capitalism, big corporations spend millions advertising these junk foods. All they care about is profit, baby!

My wife and I don't buy much in the junk food aisle at the supermarket. But whenever I'm there, the choices of chip products and other junk foods catch my attention. The portions are larger than ever. These guys make junk food so inviting, and people keep buying. Now, because of lack of time to make proper meals, a high accumulation of processed sugar, high fructose corn syrup, and too many carbs, and our sedentary lifestyle, we are all battling weight problems.

Now is the best time to make some changes. Start making your food decisions based on the amount of water and high fructose corn syrup in your food. Eat foods with more water, and stay away from foods with high fructose corn syrup. Be more physically active. A twenty-minute walk every day will add years to your life.

Start with small, consistent steps, and these healthy habits will soon become a normal part of your life. We will elaborate more on these decisions in the following lettered exits. However, this is the first thing you need to do now: if you use processed white sugar, stop using it. The next time you go to the store, buy a bottle of Agave, real maple syrup, honey, and Stevia. Agave is an all-natural sugar product from the agave plant. We buy a bottle of agave every other month, and have not needed white sugar in the house for years. Stevia is ten times as strong as white sugar. It's all natural, and also comes from a plant. We bought a Stevia plant a couple inches tall at a nursery last spring. By autumn, it was two feet tall. The leaf is unbelievably sweet. It's an awesome plant to add to your garden. You can also buy Stevia extract, but remember to use it very sparingly, because it is very strong. We don't eat desserts, so we don't really need sweeteners that much. I use a splash of Agave when making salad dressing and use real maple syrup on French toast.

Here's one easy habit to break: stop putting hundreds of calories in your coffee by adding huge amounts of cream and sugar. Drink it black, or get into green tea. Forget the wimpy "light and sweet" coffee or tea. Get your calories from "real" food. Typically, real food has fewer calories than sugar. Meanwhile, half of the time, that stuff you use to whiten your coffee isn't even cream—it's some kind of chemical!

Memories of exit 3A

- Stop using white sugar. Instead, try some agave, honey, real maple syrup, or Stevia.
- Think about the amount of water in the foods you eat.
- Become more active and get moving.

Speaking of cream, try listening to “I Feel Free” by the band Cream.

EXIT 4

THE MENU OF DISTRACTION

Being distracted while driving is the biggest cause of accidents. Some people surround themselves with lots of distractions, and to top it off, they move at an excessive speed at the same time.

In the beginning the automobile was just a steel frame, body, and four tires. It had a gas pedal for acceleration, a brake pedal for halting motion, and a steering wheel for changing direction. Engineers have unbelievably improved the automobile in every possible aspect in the last one hundred years. Ninety years ago, my father had a Model T Ford. Every winter night, he used to drain the oil, drain the water, take out the battery, and bring them all in. He'd put them near the wood stove, so the car would run the next day.

Nowadays, most vehicles are safe, luxurious, spacious, efficient, and comfortable. Really, they're high-tech rocket ships loaded with computer chips. Even though vehicles are so advanced these days, when I drive five hundred miles, I come across some pretty wacky scenarios. When I see terrible accidents, I constantly wonder, *How the hell did that happen?*

It makes me remember that the automobile is a serious killer. Most people don't realize it, but driving is about the most dangerous thing you do everyday. The problem is that, for most of us, it's done automatically, by habit, without thought. Being that it's a learned habit—like riding a bike—and because of the ego part, everybody thinks they are a great driver. It's really difficult to teach people how to be a better driver, because they think they're great at it already.

With the number of deaths and injuries that happen on a daily basis on our roads, I think people are so used to driving that they think it's a freaking video game. I really don't care that almost no one wants to learn how to drive; I am going to teach the few who do care.

No one is really paying attention when they are driving, because it's such a habit. The authorities try to make laws to ensure people become more attentive—these new laws really amaze me. They state that it is illegal to hold an electronic device in your hand while driving. However, it's okay to change the heater or AC setting, or look at someone in the passenger or back seat. It's okay to talk, tune the radio, eat and drink, and look for street signs or house numbers.

At sixty miles per hour, you travel eighty-eight feet in one second. A lot can go wrong in a second. You need to know that, despite the laws, people still don't pay attention when driving. Sadly, this also includes you. But, unlike what many people think, you *can* allow for a little distraction at a safe time. Let me explain. If you're on the interstate, and you want to change a Bluetooth setting, don't you think it'll be best to do it when you aren't driving close to another car? Accelerate out, isolate yourself from other drivers, and then get distracted for a second or so. It's common sense, but sadly, it's not so common.

I can make a very long list of scenarios where you should never get distracted. The most important ones include: poor visibility situations, residential areas where children could possibly be playing, areas with many side streets, in heavy traffic, and especially when you have other people in the car trying to tell you what to do. As earlier mentioned, there will always be distractions, but it's better to choose when to get distracted. Choosing increases your odds of staying safe.

In this digital era, I think "rear-end accidents" in heavy traffic have greatly increased. Talking and texting while driving is dangerous. The morning and evening sun, which tend to impair the vision of people driving east and west in the morning and evenings respectively, also play dangerous roles. When you are driving during rush hour, when cars are trailing each other closely at sixty or seventy miles per hour, you should stay a couple inches to the left. This way, you can see the sides of the car in front of you, and the brake lights of vehicles six or eight cars ahead.

Check your mirrors often, so you know if you have a way out if necessary. Do not follow closely behind large trucks, vans, SUVs, or any car bigger than yours. It is quite difficult to see around these cars. Instead, release the gas and lag behind a little so you can stay a couple car lengths away from them. Remember to focus on "getting the big picture."

A friend of mine who is a State Trooper told me that whenever there is an accident, quite often another one happens close by. This is because everyone wants to see the accident, so while driving past the accident scene, they switch their attention from the road to the wreck. They call it "rubbernecking," because your neck is like a piece of rubber as you look around. This often results in another accident.

If you must look at that accident scene or anything else, remember to leave some space between you and other cars. It doesn't matter if another car overtakes you or cuts in. Just stay safe, and be on guard by constantly doing a brake cover. Many people are wondering what's going on, and they're not paying attention to anything else. Don't be like them. At this point, you may want to check out Marvin Gaye's famous song "What's Going On."

Memories of Exit 4

- Life is full of choices; get yourself in a safer situation by choosing when to entertain distractions.
- Keep those eyes moving, constantly looking for danger.

EXIT 4A

"KEEP ON GROWING" DEREK AND THE DOMINOS IF I COULD ONLY HUSTLE YOU INTO PLANTING A GARDEN...

We all have to eat and drink to stay alive, but do you ever think about where all this food and water come from? Obviously, the water in your sink comes from a well, reservoir, aquifer, etc. We are lucky that we have a water cooler and can fill up the jugs at a spring in Saratoga State Park. Bottled water is a billion-dollar business but certain bottled water brands are simply town water run through a fancy filter system. And what about the food you eat? How far did it travel to get to you? How much processing or preservatives were involved? What about refrigeration, packaging, and canning? Did they add some additives and genetically modified organisms (GMOs), or is it purely organic?

Have you ever paused to think about all these questions? We need to all start thinking a little more about the processes our food went through before getting to us. Thanks to the growing popularity of farmers' markets, more people are beginning to buy foods locally. One big advantage of buying food at a farmers' market is that you are dealing directly with the person who grew the food, so you can learn from them by asking questions. We have learned quite a few tips about growing veggies by talking to farmers at these markets. On that note, why not try to grow some food, even if it's just a parsley plant on the windowsill?

Years ago, I was not into gardening, but interacting with those farmers sparked my interest. First I built a couple of raised beds for my wife, and gradually, our interest in gardening kept growing. Gardening is one of the easiest fun things to do; all you need is seeds, a pot, dirt, sun, and some water. You can infuse some variations to it, but these are the basic things you need. Try growing something. It's fun. There are quite a few vegetables that are very easy to grow. If you have any young children around, you should grow some sugar snap peas. They're fun to eat right off the vine. As I am writing this, it's early November. We just planted about 500 to 600 garlic cloves! Yes, you plant garlic by this time of year, up here in New York.

We have lived in Wilton, New York (near Saratoga) for around 25 years. We are very lucky to have a very level piece of property. You can get a truck right to the garden. In our area, the soil is very sandy, so in order to have a good garden you have to add nutrients. We typically bring in a pickup truck of cow manure every other year. We also have a twenty-five-year-old rotting leaf pile that turns into black gold compost when you dig down into it. We use it as soil for the garden.

We currently have about 20 raised beds, around four feet by five feet. Deb recently started saying that enough is enough. Sometimes, she complains that we grow too much of this and not enough of that. Typically, too many hot peppers and tomatoes and not enough swiss chard and beets.

The weather determines how each year's gardening activity turns out. This past year, we had a hail storm in May that beat us up pretty bad, killing many plants. Most years we grow an abundance of wonderful veggies. I currently start some plants indoors with a few grow lights; someday we will have a small greenhouse.

My gardening plans for the spring would be to grow many more flowers in the backyard. What about you? What's your gardening plan? If you don't have any, I encourage you to start growing something, even if it's a tiny herb plant on a windowsill. It could be vegetables or flowers. Vegetables are good for you, and they're expensive to buy. Why not save money by growing some? All you need is some good soil, sun, and water. You can also use something as simple as a bag. Buy a bag of potting soil, throw it in a sunny spot in your yard, cut off the top, punch a bunch of holes through the whole bag with a long screwdriver, plant some seeds, water them once in a while, and you're off to a great start.

If you don't live in a place where you can grow anything, it's not a bad idea to find a farmers' market in your area. Support those local farmers and eat fresh and local produce. If you don't have a farmers' market in your area, at least be conscious of what aisles in the supermarket you do most of your shopping in. Everyone has different eating habits. I don't know what your habits are, but a great tip is to start your shopping in the produce section.

Set a goal of eating a handful of nuts and some fresh fruit every day. Start today, by buying an apple, some berries, oranges, or grapes. Every other evening, I slice up an apple, peel it, cut it into chunks, and throw it in a container with a few shakes of cinnamon. I put it in the fridge to take to work for a snack the next day. I use nuts as my go-to snack—eating a handful of nuts everyday is a great way to increase your fiber intake and lower your cholesterol. I have read that over half of Americans do not get enough fiber in their diet, this info is from Health.Harvard.edu. This is because people eat a lot of fast food, which is mostly highly processed and filled with chemicals, salt, and sugar-laden garbage. If you constantly carry a bunch of good foods with you during the day, it will help you resist the urge to buy and eat garbage.

Other times, I slice up different colored peppers, celery, and cucumbers, and eat them during the day, dipped in hummus or guacamole. Doing things like this can help wean you off the fast-food chain addiction, if you have it. Another great idea is to buy a mint plant, some potting soil, and a pot. Plant it—this way, whenever you make lemonade, you can grab a couple fresh mint leaves as a garnish. You can even add some vodka and make some fresh mojitos.

The most exciting thing about gardening is how much everything changes day by day, during the growing season. First, you see little sprigs popping out of the ground; then you see the first true leaves. Pretty soon, you start to see flowers, then tiny little veggies. You would really be amazed at how fast some veggies grow. Your zucchini could be three inches long today, and by tomorrow, it would be almost a foot. Now imagine the fun of having a different veggie ready to pick on any given day. Imagine giving away cucumbers, zucchini, tomatoes, etc., because you have way too many. Start today. Buy a pot, get some dirt, plant some seeds, or buy a small plant, and grow something.

Recently, on July 4th, we picked the first head of garlic. Garlic is so easy to grow, it's like child's play. We planted it around Halloween week, and now we're already picking it. It is one of the easiest things to grow. Choose an area with a decent amount of sun, clear away the grass, loosen up the dirt, and add some organic materials. Stick your finger in the ground, put in a clove of hard-stem garlic, cover it with a little dirt, and throw some leaves over it. By mid-April, you will see a shoot coming up. Do a little weeding and water it a few times weekly. By mid-July, it'll be ready for harvest.

As you get older, there is a good chance you are going to become interested in gardening. You might as well jump on it now and start a little earlier. Our song recommendation for this exit is Derek and the Dominos song, "Keep on Growing."

Memories of Exit 4A

- Grow something.
- Start small. Buy a parsley plant and put it in a sunny windowsill.
- You can grow a lot of greens and herbs with a grow light system.
- Shop in that produce aisle a little more.
- Stop by a farmers market for some fun!

EXIT 5

COMPARED TO WHAT?

I was bummed out because I didn't have any shoes, then I met a man with no feet. This old adage simply means that in life, everything is relative. We all react to feelings or situations by comparing them to something else. Our sense of judgment is deeply intertwined with our past experiences. Let me ask you something again: are you a finished product or a work in progress? I believe most people would answer "work in progress," because we all want to believe we still have the ability to learn. After all, deep down in our psyche, we all are striving for a better life.

I always love the old shoe salesman story. Here's an abridged version of it. About a hundred years ago, a thriving shoe factory in upstate New York sent two salesmen to a large, third-world country halfway around the world. The first salesman wrote letters back, saying, "Forget it, I am coming back home.There is no market here, no one wears shoes." The second salesman wrote back saying, "Hurry, buy more property. We will have to build a way bigger factory. It is going to be fantastic. No one wears shoes, no one sells shoes. We are going to sell thousands of pairs."

If you are a work in progress, you must have a thought or vision of the person you want to be. Hopefully that person is filled with faith, hope, generosity, humility, serenity, excitement, and all the other positive traits a human can have. The next time you react to a situation, instead of reacting as the person you are at the moment, react to it as the person you want to be. I know, it's a tough task in this fast-paced society, but you can do it. First, try to slow things down a bit and be a little more mellow. Then, ask yourself how the person you want to be will react to this situation.

This is what works for me: whenever I find myself reacting hastily to a situation, I look at one of my fingernails. This reminds me that I can "nail" this by taking an extra moment to think before reacting. Remember, you're "a work in progress," so it may take some time to perfect this. The hard part is trying to remember to relax and think before reacting. Always remember, it's not what happens to you in life that matters, but how you react to it. You can laugh, or cry—it's up to you to decide. Slow down and relax for a minute, then ensure that you react like the person you want to be.

We all have problems, that's life. Imagine if you were in a room with twenty people, where everyone wrote down their problems and threw them in a basket. Now imagine that you could pick any problem instead of yours. Guess what? There are high chances you would want yours back. After you've read all their problems, you would look at yours in a different light.

Remember Pavlov's dogs? If you ring a bell and then feed a dog a bunch of times, the dogs will automatically start salivating whenever they hear the bell ring. We humans are the same way. We all make far too many impulsive and automatic decisions. You are where you are today because of many impulsive decisions you made in the past. Think about all these little decisions a bit more—take your time. When someone asks you an important question, a great way to slow things down is to say, "Let me think about it for a minute," before you speak. It doesn't make you dull. It only helps you get the right answers and decisions. It also gives you the time to compare your regular answer or reaction to how the person you want to be would answer or react. There is a great jazz song called "Compared to What" performed by Les McCann and Eddie Harris at the 1969 Montreux Jazz Festival. Find it on YouTube. The intro is a little long, but after that, the lyrics bear a powerful message.

Memories of Exit 5

- Think before you speak.
- Always remember: it is not what happens to you in life that matters; it is how you react to what happens to you.
- Life is relative; "compared to what?"

EXIT 5A

MORE WATER!

I constantly talk about eating foods with more water, eating fewer processed foods, eating more veggies, and eating more fiber. Meanwhile, I am not the "man of steel." I hate to admit it, but I make tons of eating mistakes. Yes, I eat at Jersey Mike's (Big Kahuna). I eat at Five Guys (small cheeseburger and, sadly, no fries). I eat pizza, Taylor Ham egg and cheese, and bagels with veggie cream cheese when I'm in Jersey. I do love a bar lunch, chicken wings, BLTs, cold beer, etc. (I was brought up Catholic, so this is like a confession session to me.) My eating mistakes are one of the main reasons I like to make soup whenever I get time, to ensure I eat enough veggies, and to get more water.

Today, for instance, Deb and I had a dish of broccoli soup. It was delicious and easy to make. All you need is a cutting board, a halfway decent knife, a potato peeler, potato masher, a pot, and a stove. The ingredients include one or two heads of broccoli, a box of chicken broth or stock, two to three cloves of garlic, two to three potatoes, and a chunk of sharp cheddar.

You start by pouring a quart (32 oz.) of chicken broth or stock into at least a three-quart pot and turning on the heat. Wash the head of broccoli, chop it into one-inch chunks (including stem), and add to the pot. Peel the potatoes, chop into one-inch chunks, and add it to the pot. Crush your garlic with a knife or garlic press, and add to the pot. After fifteen or twenty minutes, poke the potatoes with a fork to make sure they are done. If they are, take a potato masher and mash the contents to the texture you like. You could also use an immersion blender to get an even texture. If the soup is too thick, add more broth, stock, water, or white wine. If it's too watery, don't fret. The cheese you add will make it thicker. At this point, chop or grate the cheddar cheese and melt it into the soup, small portions at a time

When you are done with this, you can then add salt and freshly ground pepper to taste, and enjoy. If you don't like broccoli, you can make this soup with any other veggies, like mushrooms, onions, leeks, carrots, asparagus, squash, zucchini, etc. You can also garnish it with fresh parsley, chopped scallion, chopped jalapeno, finely chopped red onion, grating cheese, or maybe a swirl of sour cream or heavy cream.

This delicious meal can go with garlic bread. To make, slice some Italian bread however you like it and put in a baking pan. Crush 4 cloves of garlic, and put them in a bowl with a few tablespoons of olive oil or melted butter. Add a few tablespoons of good grating cheese. You can also add some chopped red onion or jalapeno if you wish. Stir the mixture and set aside. Take the pan of Italian bread and put it in the broiler. At this point you really can't be doing anything else. You have to pay attention to toasting the bread, as it will burn very easily. Keeping an eye on the bread, toast it to a light brown. Turn the bread over, depending how you cut it, and repeat.

Remove the bread from the broiler and spread the mixture generously on it. Then, return it to the broiler for one minute. Again, pay close attention, and don't let it burn. When it's done, remove it from the broiler and enjoy. You can pair it with a bottle of red or white wine, and, if there are any leftovers, this soup gets better the next day. Try listening to the Billy Joel song, "Scenes from an Italian Restaurant," bottle of red, bottle of white.

Memories of Exit 5A

- Try to always choose the food with more water.

EXIT 6

ARE YOU CONNECTED?

Every driver has an element of fear in them. In certain cases, fear is healthy because driving is actually life-threatening. Whenever we strap ourselves behind the wheel, we put our life on the line. But then, it's important to have a healthy level of confidence and feel secure behind the wheel. When you are driving, it's important to have the conviction that every move you make is the right move. You can overcome the fear of the unknown by having a good understanding of your own driving habits and their limitations.

The path to understanding your habits and building greater confidence begins by putting things into practice. The truth is, you have to make lightning-fast decisions if you are going to drive safely. At every point, you must quickly decide if you should steer, accelerate, or brake. These decisions are typically impulsive, so you have to have enough knowledge and experience to decide right.

Reading this book will improve your driving because it will stimulate your thought process, but remember, a larger part of driving depends on your impulse and habits. You can't change those habits by merely reading a book. You have to put the things you've read into practice and imprint them in your brain, to reset your automatic reactions.

Imagine driving along an interstate on a beautiful sunny day, when all of a sudden you see brake lights up ahead and tons of flashing red lights. As you slow down and sit in traffic for a minute, you suddenly see an upside down SUV in the median with car parts strewn around. You start wondering what could have happened. Here's typically what happened: someone was not paying attention or dozed off, and all of a sudden they found themselves running off the road doing seventy-five miles per hour.

Firstly, it is very dangerous to drive when you are drowsy or tired. The only solution is to pull into a rest area and take a nap, rather than getting in a wreck and hurting someone.. One thing you can do that will help you stay awake a little bit is always carry water and paper towels. Put some water on towels and wet your face, big time. Another trick is to chew gum or eat something. Blast the radio and sing, or open all the windows and stick your head out for a minute. If you have a hands-free phone set up, call someone and talk for a while. While all these are a temporary fix, the only solution I really recommend is that you should pull into a rest area and take a nap.

When people doze off and suddenly find themself skidding off the road, they get startled and whip the wheel too fast to the left or right. This sudden and extreme weight transfer makes them lose control of the car, causing it to flip over. Now, the right thing to do if you ever find yourself in this situation would be to hold on to the wheel, go straight a bit, slow down, and regain control. Then, gently steer back onto the road. You must always have it at the back of your mind that the steering wheel can be dangerous, if you make an abrupt move on it. This is particularly worse if you're driving a vehicle that sits up a little higher, like an SUV.

Vehicles are heavy, and there are limits to how quickly they can change direction. An object going in a straight line wants to keep going in a straight line. If you force it to change direction abruptly, the tires will possibly lose adhesion—or, if the center of gravity is too high, it could possibly flip over.

Only experience will really teach you how to control your steering in certain situations. Reading isn't sufficient to teach you how to control your steering when, for instance, your brakes are locked on a slippery surface. You have to experience it for yourself so you know the sensation, and know how to remedy it. However, here's a little exercise that'll teach you how to drive when the roads are covered in snow. Drive to the biggest parking lot you know, and find a deserted area. Drive in a straight line at twenty miles an hour, then slam on the brakes. While on your brakes, and the car is skidding, try to steer. You will find out that moving the steering wheel means nothing. Do it a bunch of times, and realize that you can only steer if you get your legs off the brakes.

Now, pretend that you are going around a turn—that is, steering to the left—and in the middle of the turn, you slam the brakes. You'll notice that the car will start going straight. Whenever it snows, do this exercise as many times as possible so you can imprint in your brain to stay off the brakes when trying to turn. While you are in that parking lot, smash the gas pedal and feel what happens. There is a huge difference with what happens depending on if the vehicle is in front-wheel drive, rear-wheel drive or all-wheel drive. Typically, you will still go straight ahead with front-wheel drive or all-wheel drive, but if you have rear-wheel drive, the rear end will go left or right when you break traction. Remember, steer where you want to go. Do these kinds of things as much as possible so you know the remedy when it happens unexpectedly.

It's essential to learn how to drive on slippery roads during the winter; however, when it starts to rain, the roads can also be extremely slippery as the oil in the asphalt loosens up a little bit. In this kind of situation, slow down, and don't be too aggressive with the steering, brake, or gas pedal. Try to remember that when there is moisture on the road and the temperature is below freezing; it being slippery could catch you off guard.

Habitually, your brain has been wired to always step on the brakes whenever it seems like you're losing control. But when you lose control on a slippery surface, stepping on the brakes is actually the worst thing you could do. You will be much better off using the steering wheel and turning in the direction you want to go. When you are driving in winter conditions, you are usually in the "groove" other cars have made in the snow ahead of you. If you begin to move left or right into the three- or four-inch snow, many people will hit the brakes, which will make things worse.

Instead of braking, here's what you should do when you start hitting the deeper snow: give it a little gas, and steer where you want to go in very small increments. While doing this, keep steering straight as you're looking for traction. Don't fret. Relax and maintain control while you gently steer back into the groove, or center of your lane. Practice at slower speeds on a lesser traveled road whenever you can.

When you are traveling on a three-lane interstate in a blizzard, following someone at a safe distance in the middle lane in the groove, try to relax—even if you are running late. I would not recommend being the asshole that goes over in the fresh snow on another lane just to go faster. Statistically, these are the people who run off the road the most. And they usually have four-wheel drive. What most people don't realize is that four-wheel drive vehicles are not magically super safe when driving in a blizzard. Their front tires can lose traction and skid, just like any other vehicle. It's just that the people with four-wheel drive are overconfident. Also, it's important to note that four-wheel drive means nothing in terms of stopping, compared to two-wheel drive. When driving on a slippery surface, do all your braking while moving in a straight line. Stay off the brakes when turning and please slow down when it is slippery.

One important factor that we mustn't neglect is the condition of your tires. An automobile is connected to the road by only four little tire patches, each only a little bit bigger than the size of two sticks of butter. It's really amazing to realize what a car is capable of with only that tiny, yet crucial, connection. If your tires are worn out and you drive in the snow or rain, you are asking for major trouble. If you know you need new tires, slow down in the rain—otherwise, your tires may easily hydroplane (float up on top of the water with no control). If you have a bad tire, it can also make the car shimmy and shake. Even if you're broke, replace your worn tires before winter. Doing so will save you money in the long run.

Where I used to work, all the trailer tires were checked for pressure every day. The pressure must be 110 pounds—meanwhile, we were carrying 12,000 gallons of gas. We once had a manager who was trying to save money by buying cheap Chinese recaps. The tires were constantly blowing up while we transported the goods. It was so annoying, stranded on the side of an interstate with a blown tire and 12,000 gallons of gas, while other cars zoomed by at seventy-five miles per hour. He eventually got fired, and the next manager bought new Michelins for all the trailers. It was expensive, but it fixed our tire problems for a good while. Quality, which is hard to find these days, always beats price.

If you ever own or use a trailer, ensure you always buy the highest quality tire you can possibly buy. Check your tire pressure often so you don't get stuck on the road. If you own a boat trailer or camper that you don't use regularly, bear in mind that letting it sit idle at one spot will damage the tire eventually. Remember to always check for "dry rot" (small cracks).

One more piece of information: if you drive a different vehicle in the winter, always remember that wider tires tend to ride up on top of the snow, where a thinner tire will cut the snow. Try listening to the first Kenny Rogers hit, "Just Dropped In (To See What Condition My Condition Was In)."

Memories from Exit 6

- Do not drive if you are tired.
- In the winter, get all your braking done while you're going in a straight line.

- The brakes are not always your savior.
- Buy new, high-quality tires when your existing tires show signs of wear. The condition of your tires becomes much more important when the roads are wet or if it's snowing. Tires are the only thing connecting you to the road.
- Check your tire pressure more often, and make sure you check your trailer tires for tire pressure and dry rot before that vacation trip.

EXIT 6A

A LITTLE GARLIC, A LITTLE OLIVE OIL

Around here, we make a tomato sauce we call a "quick sauce." It's primarily used to eat some type of pasta, but you can really put it on anything. It's typically a marinara, but you could also add meat, shrimp, clams, whatever. Today I started with a few tablespoons of olive oil and a pat of butter in a sauté pan on very low heat. I added three cloves of garlic, crushed in a garlic press. While that was starting to sauté, I started very finely chopping a bunch of veggies. I chopped a small amount of carrots, onion, a celery stalk, a few slices of sweet red pepper, and hot pepperoncini. I brought a slice of meatloaf leftover from the night before and around four or five Kalamata olives I had in the fridge. To that, I added a few ounces of red wine cabernet sauvignon, and a twenty-eight-ounce can of crushed tomatoes. I let that sauté for about fifteen minutes (hence quick sauce). Then, I poured it on top of some frozen ravioli I had cooked earlier, poured a glass of wine for Deb and myself, got out the grating cheese, fresh parsley and the crushed hot red pepper—and voilà! We had the time of our lives. Alternatively, you can also add a heavy splash of Vodka and four ounces of heavy cream. As the liquid content reduces while cooking, you can add another splash of white wine.

Let me tell you a few things about grating cheese. The best grating cheese in the world is Parmigiano-Reggiano. It is "Reggiano" because it comes from a certain area of Italy called Parma-Reggio. It is made from cow's milk. It is a very expensive cheese, costing about fifteen or twenty dollars a pound, but it's worth every penny. When I'm feeling rich, I buy a chunk and grate it at home. The cheese we use daily is a Romano. It is made from sheep's milk, and it's not as expensive as the Reggiano. We typically only buy one brand called Locatelli, which is also from Italy. Both of these cheeses are known to be the best grating cheeses in the world. Most of the grating cheeses made in America cannot compare with those from Italy. When you read the ingredients list, many of them contain cellulose (ground up wood chips) as an additive.

Here's another delicious, quick sauce you can use for your pasta or any other meal: Crush some garlic in a press, and finely chop a shallot. Get a quarter stick of butter, chop a few anchovies, and add a healthy splash of olive oil and a splash of white wine. Throw them all in a little sauté pan on low heat. In another pan, cook your pasta of choice. When it's done, drain and toss it into the sauté pan. Add huge amounts of good grating cheese and enjoy. Don't forget to add some crushed red pepper and salt to taste.

Get creative with your meals. You can incorporate chicken broth, chopped veggies, fresh tomatoes in season, shrimp, clams, salmon, salami, sausage, lobster, bacon, etc. Here's another red sauce recipe you should try.

Start by crushing four to five cloves of garlic and sautéing it in olive oil on low heat for five to ten minutes. Add either three or four anchovies (crushed) or a teaspoon of anchovy paste to the mixture. Add a finely chopped shallot and sauté for another couple of minutes. At this point, add a quarter pound of finely chopped salami, chopped red pepper, a cup of dry red wine, and a large can of good, Italian, crushed tomatoes. Sauté this mixture on low while you get your pasta ready.

When your pasta is done, drain and dish it out. Then, add this delicious sauce and garnish with a generous portion of grating cheese and a healthy shake of crushed red pepper. Throw some Italian bread in the oven, pour a nice glass of merlot, and enjoy. Don't forget to get creative with this meal. If you're using canned tomatoes, I recommend San Marzano. Just a note on these tomatoes, they are whole, so you have to break them up with your hands or put them in the blender. They're also from Italy, and I promise you, they are the best canned tomatoes in the world. Talking about promises, YouTube the Eric Clapton song "Promises."

Memories of Exit 6A

- Stop buying jarred red sauce. Make your own, instead.
- Experiment with different versions; it's fun and very tasty.
- Once in a while, splurge and buy a chunk of the best grating cheese in the world, Parmigiano-Reggiano, and grate it yourself.
- While you are splurging, buy a chunk of Locatelli, it's Romano made from sheep's milk.

- Try San Marzano canned tomatoes. They're expensive, but not as expensive as eating out. Just a note: San Marzano tomatoes have to be from a certain area in Italy; "San Marzano Style" could be tomatoes from anywhere.

EXIT 7

TOP TEN HITS!

I can't remember where I saw this list, but it was so profound that I jotted it down at the back of one of my spiral notebooks. It's a list of ten ways to live a longer and happier life. Just for the record, I'm seventy-four, so if you're younger, you may want to pay attention. Here they are:

1. Get a colonoscopy. (I've had one ten years ago, and I am scheduled for another one next month. By the time of publication, I must have done it.)
2. Stop eating before you are full (I am not very good at this).
3. Use sunscreen (I never used it, but I do stay away from the sun).
4. Stop smoking. (I quit nine years ago, when a great doctor told me I had to quit if I wanted to stay alive, as it was wrecking my vascular system. After quitting, they had to clean both of my carotid arteries.)
5. Sleep a lot. (Thank God, I am pretty good at this one.)

6. Move! (I think I do this quite well. Although I did drive a truck for a living, I used to walk around the truck five to ten times about thrice daily instead of just sitting. This has been quite helpful. Today, I'm just ten pounds overweight. I am an avid gardener and I love shoveling snow. I have also downloaded the "Fitbit" app on my phone, and I try to walk 10,000 steps every day.)
7. Eat fresh produce. (I believe I am above average at this. I have already shared how I eat a lot of vegetables and other fresh meals.)
8. Floss. (I can't do this because I have all false teeth.)
9. Cultivate healthy relationships. (I have also shared how we often invite family and friends to hang out and have dinner with us. Remember, I am a famillionaire!)
10. Be grateful. (I cannot overemphasize this. I consider it the pillar of my existence.)

I am going to add a few things to the list that I think are of utmost importance. First off, SMILE! In previous exits, I have already explained how smiling does a lot of good to your body and soul.

Another important concept is to be mindful of your tribe. By "tribe" I mean the people you hang out with. They can have a very big effect on your life. Remember, you are the average of the five people you spend most of your time with. If you hang out with a bunch of crybabies and complainers, odds are you are going to be one. If you hang out with a bunch of creative, happy, good-attitude people, odds are you are going to be the same. Don't be part of a bad tribe. If you are, this is the time to withdraw from them and get a new tribe of positive-minded folks. You are who you hang out with. If your tribe doesn't have the kind of virtues you need, but you want to keep them anyway, then you have to start teaching them to be positive. You are helping them, but while at it, ensure they're not people who suck away your energy and happiness.

Here's another: Stop collecting possessions, and start collecting experiences. As you get older, you will start to realize you have too much stuff already, and you really don't need it all. This is quite a sensitive topic because some people love being collectors. But just as you're advised to say no to drugs, I'm advising you to say no to junk. My wife has had so many garage sales; even so, sadly, we couldn't sell some of our junk. Experiences, on the other hand, can be stored in your brain. If you don't like them, they are very easy to throw out.

Hence, gather lots of experiences, and hold on to the ones that make you happy. Here's something I came across that Steve Jobs said: "Your work is going to fill a large part of your life, and the only way to be truly satisfied is to do what you believe is truly great work. And the only way to do truly great work is to love what you do. If you haven't found it yet, keep looking. Don't settle, as with all matters of the heart, you'll know when you find it, and like any great relationship, it just gets better and better as the years roll by."

As I have already said several times, never give up. Don't give up on your dream. Keep working on it, and stay motivated. If you work on something for an hour every day, for five years, you can become an expert. Even when you lack motivation, just keep working for the purpose of helping others. As Henry Ford said, "If you believe you can, or believe you can't, either way you're right!" I saw a documentary of an interview with Bob Hoover, a very famous test pilot who was still doing tricks with airplanes around the world in his seventies. When asked what his secret was, he said, whenever someone said this or that was impossible, he didn't believe them. Instead, he found ways to show that it was possible.

To get off this exit, listen to one of the greatest male vocalists of all time, Luther Vandross, sing "The Impossible Dream" (from Always and Forever: An Evening of Songs at The Royal Albert Hall).

Memories of Exit 7

- Stop collecting possessions; start collecting experiences and memories.
- Always find reasons to never give up. If your reason is big enough, you can always stay motivated.

EXIT 7A

PING-PONG

Let's start off this exit by teaching you a meatball recipe I have fine-tuned after talking to many Italian chefs over the years. Whenever you eat at a restaurant, don't be afraid to ask questions. Sometimes, the chef will come out and talk to you. A chef typically loves to talk to people about food. I happen to like meatballs that are a little softer or lighter than ordinary.

Here's how to make it: You need to buy a few pounds of meatloaf mix. This mixture is typically one third beef, one third pork, and one third veal. Meatloaf mix has more flavor than just chopped meat. Start by soaking three or four slices of white bread or a chunk of Italian bread in a bowl. Pour half a cup of half-and-half, soak them together, and ensure the bread has the consistency of cottage cheese. Add finely chopped carrots and about five cloves of crushed garlic. Add the meatloaf mix and one egg to the bowl and mix thoroughly. Add some chopped onions or a shallot, some fresh parsley, and a quarter cup of Locatelli grating cheese. Mix thoroughly, and add more half-and-half if the mixture looks dry.

Form them into meatballs the size of a ping-pong ball, and bake in the oven for twenty minutes. Remove from the oven, add to quick sauce with drippings (Exit 6A) and simmer on low heat for at least an hour. Don't forget to add some red wine, a peeled carrot, and a half an onion to the sauce. For more excitement you can add a piece of browned sausage, pork chops, or chicken breasts. If you want to change the quick sauce recipe a bit, you could start it with chopping some onions, carrots, and celery in a pot of water or chicken broth, and boiling them for an hour or until very soft *(mirepoix)*. Use your immersion blender to mix thoroughly, then add it to the sauce.

There was a very famous Italian restaurant in New York City years ago called Mama Leones. It closed down in 1994. They served 700,000 meals a year in eleven dining rooms. I was never able to go there, but I read in her cookbook that she always added some pats of butter to her sauce.

Cook some pasta of your choice (add a splash of olive oil). You should always try new shapes of pasta, just to make it fun (add a couple ounces of the pasta water to your sauce). After that, throw some Italian bread in the oven, add your grating cheese, put out some nice olives and your garlic butter, and enjoy your meal with a Cab, Merlot, Chianti, or a Pinot noir. If there are leftovers, the next day you could make a quick shrimp scampi and add it to the sauce. You could throw in a can of clams, a lobster tail, some heavy cream, and a few splashes of vodka. And please don't forget, you can chop any kind of veggie and add it to the sauce or meatballs.

Go on YouTube and search for the song "Hey, Good Lookin'" by Hank Williams.

Memories of Exit 7A

- Make some homemade meatballs and sauce, and add a little butter.
- The next day, you can add anything you like to the left-overs—maybe a small can of black olives, a splash of chicken broth, and a splash of wine?

EXIT 8

DA PRE TRIP

A syndicated radio show called "Car Talk" is hosted by a couple of guys from Boston who answer questions about cars and other mechanical stuff. My concept of "car talk" is a little different. My concept is: what would your car say if it could talk? I think it would say stuff like, "Please check my vital signs (fluid levels and tire pressure)." It would also say, "You take a shower every day. I would love a bath or shower soon," and, "Oh, you get to have a glass of coffee every day. I'd love a little extra energy once in a while too (a tank of non-ethanol super)," and, "You go to the gym now and then to workout. I'd love to get a little workout too. Floor the gas pedal at fifteen miles per hour, and let me wind up through the gears to seventy or eighty, cleaning out some carbon."

The car will also remind you that you wipe your butt every day, so it would also like some wiping (interior vacuuming). Just as you buy yourself new shoes and jeans, your car would love some new tires, new floor mats, etc. In the winter your car would be begging you to clean off all the snow before it freezes to the metal. The list could go on and on. Basically, if your car could talk, you'd hear it screaming, "HELP!" The most important thing you can do for your car is listen, because it is constantly asking for help.

In this Exit, we are going to talk about the "pre-trip." In essence, a pre-trip means to check the device to make sure it is safe to operate for the task or journey ahead. When flying an airplane, there is quite an extensive list of system checks that the pilot goes through before starting a trip.The same thing applies to driving a tractor trailer. When driving the family car, people tend to take these things for granted—but doing these pre-trip checks could help you prevent getting pulled over by the police because you have a light out or an overdue sticker.

Here are a few things I would recommend. Every day or two, walk around the car and look at the tires. An under-inflated tire looks a little bulged out at the bottom. Look out for any new scratches or dents. Look at the registration and inspection stickers and make a mental note of when they'll run out. Also, check all the lights. When you first get in the car, adjust your mirrors and ensure you're getting a good view of your back and sides. After starting the car, look at all the "idiot lights" and gauges to make sure everything is normal. When you first move, if you are backing up, look at where the car was parked to see if there are any leaks. In summer, there could be a little puddle of water—it's condensation from the air conditioning compressor, and that's normal. Instead, you look out for oily and greasy leakages.

Having dysfunctional lights is inviting the police to stop you. The easiest way to check your lights is to do it in a strip mall. When you park right in front of a store in a strip mall, you can see a reflection of your car in the big piece of glass. While you're there, check to see if your headlights are working by turning them on and off a few times.

Next, try both right and left blinkers and check if they're working. You can also back into a space in front of the store to check your taillights, brake lights, and rear signals the same way. Just recently, I taught my wife this trick at a strip mall, and I'm sure she will never forget it.

Once you turn on your car and start heading out, pay attention to any new sounds, vibrations, or pulling. Is the car tracking straight, or pulling to the left or right? Does the steering wheel feel smooth, or is it vibrating a little bit? If you notice a little shimmy or shake, it could be a sign of worn parts, a bad tire, or an unbalanced tire. When you hit the brakes, do you hear any grinding noise? If you do, you should check it out as soon as possible. That typically means your pads are worn out and you are cutting the rotor with metal. This entails that you'd be buying not only pads, but also rotors.

Do you hear a whining noise when you turn the steering wheel when you're not in motion? Your power steering fluid might be low. Do you hear a squealing sound when you first start your car? You might have a worn or loose fan belt. What about your charging system? Is it working properly? Here's a way to find out: turn on your wipers to the fastest speed. Make sure to hit the windshield washers, as it is not good to run your wipers on a dry windshield. If the wipers are a little slower than usual, your charging (read: alternator) system might not be up to par.

Nowadays there are "instant oil change" outlets everywhere. I get my oil changed at my local mechanic and, once in a while, Walmart. Our daughter bought a 2004 Honda Civic brand new. I bought it from her in 2011 with 164,000 miles on it. I drove it up to 257,000, and during this time, I changed the oil thirty times. If you use conventional oil, it's advisable to change your oil every 3000 to 4000 miles. If you use synthetic oil, which I would recommend, you can go a little further. The big piece of information here is to check your oil level every 2000 miles or so. It's best to check your oil after the car has been sitting for a while and not running. This gives all the oil a chance to drain down to the oil pan, so you can get an accurate reading. If you don't know how to check your oil, ask your mechanic and he or she will show you how.

Overheating kills a car really fast. Every car has a cooling system that circulates antifreeze through the motor, using a radiator that cools the antifreeze. The antifreeze keeps circulating, picking up heat in the motor and losing some of it when it passes through the radiator.

Without this cooling system, the car would overheat and self-destruct. This is one item that is not very forgiving. If you overheat a car, you will wreck it. Ask your mechanic or any experienced driver to show you how to check your coolant or antifreeze level. When you open the hood, there is a plastic reservoir that houses the coolant. Check it regularly to ensure that it's at the normal level. Some of the containers come with a marker on the side of the container that indicates the coolant level.

Besides feeling the steering wheel shake or hearing your brakes grinding metal to metal, you can also smell when something is wrong with your vehicle. We all know what exhaust fumes smell like, but if you smell something weird for a long period, like hot oil or evaporating antifreeze, you must quickly pull over somewhere very safe and find out what's going on. It's necessary to always check all your gauges and warning lights on the dashboard. This way, some problems won't meet you by surprise.

Do these little "pre-trip" checks every now and then, and you'll have a hitch-free trip. While at it, check out the song "Day Tripper" by The Beatles.

Memories of Exit 8

- Do a little pre-trip once in a while. Walk around the car to look at your tires and everything else.
- Clean your car regularly.
- Don't ignore any weird sound, shake, or smell.

EXIT 8A

"GO-TO FOODS"

Ask ten different people what their go-to foods are, and you will get ten different answers! It's human nature. For breakfast, some prefer Dunkin' Donuts, some have black coffee and nothing else, some people eat bagels and cream cheese, some eat a bacon, egg, and cheese sandwich. For some people, it's a Diet Pepsi, while others just want to have a piece of fruit. My go-to breakfast is either a couple quick scrambled eggs, an avocado, or a couple handfuls of berries and some whole grain crackers.

Breakfast is one thing, but lunchtime is when people really eat the craziest junk. As earlier mentioned, it's due to a dangerous combination of laziness and an inability to manage one's time. I always advise people to ditch the fast food life and fix their lunch the night before. In Exit 4A, I introduced the concept of having lunch alternatives. At the bare minimum, try to reduce the amount of bad carbs (like white bread) and processed meats you eat.

Here's a creative little recipe for one of our go-to dinners: salmon on the grill!

Start by lighting the grill. If you don't have a grill, an oven works fine, also. You have to set it at 350 for about twelve minutes. Put about one pound of salmon filet in a big piece of aluminum foil. Add an ounce or two of white wine, squeeze some lemon juice on it, sprinkle some breadcrumbs, and add some fresh dill and a healthy drizzle of real maple syrup. Close up the foil and put it on the gas grill (or oven), turning it to a low temperature for around ten to fifteen minutes.

This is an amazing and healthy dinner! It goes well with rice or quinoa and any vegetable of your choice—we like sweet potato, asparagus, broccoli, beets, or green beans. Open a nice, chilled pinot grigio and enjoy!

Another meal you should try sometime is homemade rice and beans. It's an easy, fun, healthy dish and a great way to get more beans and less meat in your diet. I have read that over 90 percent of Americans do not have enough fiber in their diet, so eating more beans is a good thing.

When food shopping, look at all the different types of rice. There's a wide variety to choose from. Try basmati, it's one of our favorites. Cook it according to the directions. While it's cooking, chop an onion, a couple of your favorite kinds of peppers, some celery, and a little carrot. Crush some cloves of garlic in your garlic press and chop some parsley to go with it. Now sauté them all in some olive oil, and add a splash of chicken broth and white wine. After sautéing for ten to fifteen minutes, throw in a few cans of beans of your choice.

Drain the rice, put it in a big pot, add the beans and veggies, throw in a can of crushed tomatoes, and you have a wonderful dinner. Pair it with a nice salad and some garlic bread. Texture is very important when talking about food. That's why it's ideal to garnish it with some "crunch," such as a few sliced scallions or a chopped jalapeño. You can also tone up the heat with a splash of Frank's RedHot. Meanwhile, don't forget to take the leftovers for lunch tomorrow.

We all need to eat more beans in our diet. My favorite quote in the book *Blue Zones* by Dan Beuttner is, "If you want to live longer, eat more plants." Here's some fun stuff, YouTube the song by Men at Work, "Down Under."

Memories of Exit 8A

- Try to get out of your eating rut. Make some changes and try something new.
- Everyone has a different go-to meal, but if you want to live longer, eat more veggies.
- The average American diet is very low in fiber. Eat more fresh veggies, fresh fruit, beans, nuts, and whole grains to get more fiber.

EXIT 9

I'M THINKING OF AN IDEA!

Some people primarily talk about other people. You would hope that when people are talking about other people, they are saying something good about the person, but we all know that's usually not the case. Other people talk primarily about things, often about all the things they have or are going to get. Some people primarily talk about ideas.

In what category do you belong? Obviously, it's okay to talk about other people positively. It's also good to have positive conversations about a thing or place. However, when you talk about ideas, you're talking about something life changing. Remember, everything begins with an idea. The wheel, the automobile, and the computer were all someone's idea. Even the refrigerator, which I consider the most important invention of the past one hundred years, started with an idea. Fifty years ago, the internet was merely someone's idea. But now look at how far it has revolutionized the world.

If you focus on thinking about ideas, you just might come up with a life changer. Think about how many lives are saved everyday by the invention of rub strips, the grooved pavement on the sides and centerline of a highway. The strips make a loud noise when you drive on them, alerting you that you are veering off the road. I'm sure it saves many lives, especially the lives of people who fall asleep or fail to pay attention when driving.

Some time ago, I read this great story about Bill Gates's mother. One day, she went into his bedroom and saw him lying on his bed. She asked, "Bill, what are you doing?" He replied, "Thinking!"

As I said earlier, if you are going to be thinking anyway, you may as well think big. You can think big about people if you are trying to make their life better, or show appreciation for their kindness. You can think big about a thing or place because it brings you some kind of positive feeling. But one thing you must always think about are ideas. Be conscious of what you always think about, and spend more time thinking of ideas rather than people or things.

Think of an idea that solves a problem. Think of doing something nice for someone. Think about smiling and not complaining for a week. Think of something fun to do to brighten your day and relieve you of stress. Think of surprising someone with a love note, a cup of coffee, or some kind of creative nice gesture.

Think of things that bring excitement and celebration into your life. Right now, I am going to celebrate that I am still working on this book, and haven't given up on it. I am going to have an ice-cold Michelob Ultra and listen to the Van Morrison song "Days Like This." Please listen to the words of this song!

Memories of Exit 9

- Think about ideas—like the idea of reading this exit again.
- Say to yourself, "I am going to come up with a life-changing idea," and realize that it is possible for you to do this, because everything begins with an idea.

EXIT 9A

CHOP, CHOP, CHOP!!!

From earlier chapters, you already know that I'm obsessed with chopping vegetables. I think it stemmed from my desire to eat foods with more water. It could also be because I just love the "chopped salad" concept that's in vogue lately.

In a food court in Montreal twenty years ago, I had a scoop of finely chopped celery and cucumbers with fresh lemon as a side with a sandwich. I squeezed on a hint of honey, and it was great. Inspired by that meal, I later made a big batch of chopped cucumbers and celery with fresh squeezed lemon, olive oil, a healthy splash of Celtic sea salt, and a squirt of Agave. I made it for a football playoff party ten years ago, so I guess I have had this obsession for a while.

If it's early evening and I am going to chop some veggies for a soup, sauce, or side, I always start with making a nice drink! Over the years, I have gotten in the habit of freezing fruit juices (with no added sugar) in ice cube trays. These fruit cubes come in handy when making a vodka drink. I do not know why, but when it comes to a vodka drink, I like a small glass around 4 oz. I simply grab a couple fruit cubes out of the freezer, add some vodka (I prefer Iceberg brand from Newfoundland) and add a squeeze of fresh lemon. Then I proceed to grab a cutting board, a sharpened knife, and a few fresh vegetables.

(Side note: It's always advisable to use wooden, composite, or plastic chopping boards. The cutting board has to be softer than the knife, so forget glass or granite—-they will wreck your knife. Technically the knife should make a small mark in the cutting board. They now make color coded cutting boards so it's an important concept, bacterium wise, to keep a separate one for meat.) Chopping vegetables is actually a healthy habit to cultivate, because whatever makes you eat more vegetables is a good thing.

Last night we made an exciting chili for dinner. We started with chopping an onion, a few stalks of celery, and some red, orange, and yellow peppers. We also chopped a few jalapeño peppers and crushed a few cloves of garlic. After letting it all simmer, we sautéed a pound of chopped meat, added a can of dark kidney beans, a can of pink kidney beans, a twelve-ounce can of tomato sauce, and all the typical chili spices. When it was all done, we served it with some good grating cheese, a splash of Frank's hot sauce and a chopped scallion garnish. The point I'm trying to make here is that you can incorporate chopped fresh vegetables into any kind of meal.

The same applies to making beef stew. To make this, we use larger chopped pieces. We will peel potatoes and chop them into roughly one-inch chunks; then, we would chop onions or shallots, then celery, carrots, and a few cloves of garlic. You see how all of these involve some chopping?

Whatever you're making for dinner, add some fresh, chopped veggies and a small chopped salad. There are so many different kinds of lettuce you can choose for your salad. Also, incorporate some thinly sliced cucumbers, some artichoke hearts, chopped carrots, and sweet red or yellow peppers. You can also add some chopped hard-boiled egg. Some other veggies you can chop and add to your salad for fun and nourishment include olives, cherry tomatoes, different-colored onions, fresh spinach, apples, cranberries, walnuts, and chunks of watermelon or mango.

When it comes to salads, forget all that bottled dressing—the only exception being Paul Newman's Italian family recipe. Why? Great ingredients, great taste, and all the profits go to charity. Make your own instead! Start with a little olive oil, add one or two drops of sesame oil, a few splashes of soy sauce, a teaspoon of good (Maille) mustard, fresh lemon juice, a clove of fresh-pressed garlic, fresh parsley, and a few drops of agave. I am not a basil fan, but if you are, chop some and add it. Mix thoroughly, pour on salad, and add chopped or crumbled cheese of your choice. You can also add extra sharp cheddar, crumbled feta, and crumbled blue cheese. Once you try this dressing, it will be your favorite for a while. Another wonderful salad dressing is a drizzle of balsamic glaze and a healthy splash of olive oil.

Another healthy meal you should try out is stuffed mushrooms. It is low carb, and is full of nutrients. This is a great dish for cleaning out the refrigerator vegetable drawer. First, you take out whatever veggies you have in that refrigerator drawer! Set a non-stick pan on the fire and add some olive oil. Chop your carrots finely and toss them into the pan. Add some finely chopped onions of your choice, and chopped sweet red orange or yellow pepper.

Next, snap the stem out of the mushrooms, chop that up, and add it. If you have any spinach that's a little too wilted for salad, chop it up and add it. Also add some black or green olives and any other leftover veggies from the drawer. While this begins to cook, stir it regularly and add a splash of chicken broth or white wine and a pat of butter.

Now, peel the mushrooms and lay them out in a cookie tray. Add a tiny pat of butter or olive oil to each one and put them in the oven at 350 for fifteen minutes, while the mixture on top of the stove is cooking. Now throw a nice splash of soy sauce on the mixture, take the mushrooms out of the oven, and put a generous tablespoon of the mixture in each mushroom. Top it with a tiny swatch of aged cheddar and return to the oven for five minutes. It's a beautiful and healthy appetizer! This is also a great mixture for stuffed flounder.

This is the basic recipe, but at the end of cooking the mixture on the stove, you can add some chopped-up shrimp, a can of clams, or chopped sausages. As always, add a splash of Frank's hot sauce if you have it.

This meal fits right into the goal of eating foods with more water, and they are delicious. If you have too much of the mixture left after filling the mushrooms, toast some bread and put it on that. Maybe that's the perfect meal you need to bring out that baby-like joy in you. Now play that Buddy Holly song from the mid-fifties titled "Maybe Baby."

Memories of Exit 9A

- Remember the Steve Miller Band song "Keep on Rock'n Me Baby?" The veggies are talking to you, saying, "Keep on choppin' me, baby."
- Add a few chopped-up, fresh veggies to your meals.

EXIT 10

CHARM SCHOOL

Imagine a scenario where you're first in line at a four-way intersection with a traffic light, and you are trying to turn left. The light turns green, but because of oncoming traffic you can't turn left. If you stay back at the line, the light might turn red again. You are not making any headway, and you are delaying everyone behind you who is trying to go straight.

What you are supposed to do is "claim the intersection" by pulling up twenty feet into the center of the intersection, moving toward the left a little, so the cars behind you that are going straight can move on from beside you. Then you wait there until the oncoming traffic stops when their light turns red, and then you can take your left.

You would think this is common sense, and everyone knows to do it, but everyday, I still see people attempting to make a left hand turn in a residential area from the center of the lane with twenty cars waiting behind them.

The same thing applies when you want to turn right in the same circumstance. It is best to stay at the extreme right side of the road, so you can make your turn without causing others to slow down when you do. If you are out in a rural area and you approach a road where you're supposed to turn, slow down, signal toward the right, and gradually shift to the extreme right. Still keep your indicator light on, so people behind you know you're turning right. That way, they will tilt away from you and keep going straight instead of slowing down.

Whenever you're at a four-way intersection, always remember the term "FIFO." It means, "first in, first out." This entails that whoever got there first has the right of way—and, of course, leaves first. In some cases, people may use a little communication in the form of a hand wave or flashing of headlights to signal they are giving up their turn and letting you go first.

And to Subaru drivers: when you are entering an interstate, press down on the right pedal a little harder. The extra lane that you are using to get on the interstate is for speeding up and merging into existing traffic. I'm so used to seeing Subaru drivers not knowing this. Sometimes when people used to ask me what I did for a living when I was driving a truck, I would answer, "I follow Subarus." Most big company tractor trailers are "governed" to sixty-five miles per hour, so when I am on the interstate doing sixty-five, typically I am following a Subaru (or maybe a Prius).

Also, always remember to keep right on those interstates. The left lanes are for overtaking. Don't just stay in that lane; you're blocking traffic. I saw a big digital sign on the Mass Pike a couple days ago that said, "Left lane for passing only, pass and move back ovah." It's arguably one of the best road signs I have seen. Some weeks back, I saw another one that said, "Driving in the left lane is only allowed when passing." I wish New York would post these signs.

I see people flouting this simple rule at least twenty times everyday on my interstate travels. You could be cruising along doing maybe seventy-three miles per hour; you're closing the gap between you and the person in front of you. You check your mirrors, go over to the left lane, and there it is: up ahead, three cars are in the slow lane and three are in the fast lane, driving right next to each other because the first car on the left isn't passing. It's just cruising on the fast lane without care.

Do you know how annoying this is? Imagine being in a checkout line at a store, and when it's your turn, you don't check out. That's exactly how annoying it is. You're wasting everyone's time. If you are ever a passenger in a car and the driver is just hanging out in the fast lane and not passing, speak up and educate them.

It truly amazes me that so many people drive like that. Is it an ego thing, where they think they can control the speed of other cars? Or is it just ignorance? I just don't get it. I guess there are certain things in life that are impossible to understand. Or maybe it's the "cows going back to the barn" syndrome. If you've been doing that, this is the best time to stop. Don't clog our already crowded highways. Hit the gas pedal, zoom pass, and return to the right.

Sometimes I think people do this because they're afraid of getting a speeding ticket. I drive over the speed limit on many interstates, all day, everyday. The typical rule of thumb is that you have to be doing twenty miles per hour over the limit to get in any trouble.

But don't get me wrong—when you see them possibly doing speed surveillance, it is always a great idea to check up and show them respect. Let's face it, the police are typically risking their lives on a daily basis to keep us safe. I would not want to go to a family dispute call when someone's pissed off, drunk, and waving a gun around—would you? Always show police the utmost respect, as they likely have a much tougher job than you do. Meanwhile, why not listen to "Fields of Gold" by Sting?

Memories of Exit 10

- When making a left at a traffic light, claim the intersection. Instead of waiting at the light, pull up twenty feet and a little to the left so other drivers can pass from beside you. That way, you won't get stuck there when the light turns red again.
- When traveling on an interstate, overtake with the left lane and keep right. Don't just cruise in the left lane next to someone.
- Try to be a little more polite and have good manners on the road. Treat people the way you'd like to be treated.

EXIT 10A

KNOW SOUP FOR YOU

It's quite hard to find any food with more water than soup. If you work in an office or have a place to heat up your soup for lunch, you are lucky and should take advantage of it. I would recommend getting a potato masher and an immersion blender. There are many delicious soups you can make if you have these items, such as broccoli cheddar and potato leek soups.

When it comes to availability, people like to rely on fast food—but they do not realize how fast and easy it is to make homemade soup. They think it takes several hours, so many don't even give it a try. Well, even if it takes a little more time to make a soup than it takes to drive by a fast food joint, what about the health implications?

Let's try something fun. Buy a rotisserie chicken at your local food store. When you get home, use a knife and fork to take out all the good meat. Chop half of the meat into smaller sizes; mix with chopped-up celery and mayo and you'll have some nice chicken salad for tomorrow.

Chop up the rest of the meat and save it for your chicken soup. Open a box of chicken broth and pour it into a pot. If you can't remember to always keep chicken or beef stock handy, buy a bottle of Better Than Bouillon and keep it in the fridge.

Slice a carrot, an onion, some celery, and three cloves of garlic. Wash and chop up two potatoes into one-inch chunks. Alternatively, you can save time by skipping the potato and throwing in some rice or pasta instead. Now throw in some chopped mushrooms and chopped fresh parsley, and you have a beautiful soup. For some exciting change, you can add a little squeeze of lemon.

For a different version, use beef broth and sausage, beef, or pork. After browning the meat in a separate pan, add a splash of white wine in the pan, scrape up the fond, and add it to your soup. Put a few splashes of Worcestershire sauce, a squeeze of tomato paste from a tube, and a squirt of soy sauce. Add spices of your choice and reduce the heat. After thirty minutes or one hour, add some cheese, olives, peppers, and Frank's hot sauce. Put some bread in the oven and crack a bottle of ice-cold beer or a nice bottle of wine. I think it would be an exciting dinner.

If you want to use shrimp, clams, or lobster in this soup, it is best to put them in when the soup is almost ready. This way, they'll only cook for a few minutes. If you cook them for too long, they'll get rubbery.

This meal is many times better than frozen pizza or a microwaved, styrofoam dinner laden with chemicals, dyes, and preservatives. Another advantage is that it doesn't contain high fructose corn syrup.

When I run out of soup ideas, or I feel like I am in a rut or have not been eating enough veggies, I go to our local bookstore and browse the cookbook section. When I find one with some new and creative soup recipes, I buy it, add it to my collection, and try some of the new ideas I have found at home. After trying a few new meals, it's fun to go on YouTube and look up how to make a couple of variations. I make a different version every couple of weeks, and enjoy a consistent supply of happy and healthy meals.

A couple hours before scripting this exit, I made a small and quick veggie soup. I poured half a box of chicken stock into a pot and added a bunch of chopped veggies like carrots, hot cherry peppers, celery, shallots, and garlic. Then I put two small potatoes and let it simmer for about 20 minutes. Then I "banged them" with the immersion blender and dished it out. Of course, I garnished the meal with lots of fresh grated Locatelli and a few slices of scallions. It's a thick, beautiful, and healthy meal better than any fast food.

Another great thing about homemade soup is that there are typically leftovers. If you ever get hungry late at night while binging around YouTube, you can heat up a few scoops of these soups and satisfy your cravings. Here's a tune I bet you have not heard in a while: "Night Shift" by the Commodores.

Memories of Exit 10A

- Make some soup. If you've never made a pot of soup, start with this easy recipe: pour a box of chicken stock in a pot, then add a couple chopped up carrots, onions, and celery. Cook the mixture on low for half an hour. Now throw in a bag of instant rice and cook for another ten minutes. Enjoy! It is actually very easy and fun. As you get more experience and confidence, put in whatever you like.

EXIT 11

EYE, EYE, ME, ME, ME, MY

Sometimes, we all get self-absorbed. It's human nature, and everyone has been guilty of it at one point or the other. We all have egos, and sometimes we want to feel important. But, as the saying goes, "God gave us two ears and one mouth for a reason." The reason is so that we can speak less and listen more. That's why it's essential to listen and pay attention sometimes, instead of always seeking to be the center of attention. Listening and paying attention to someone makes them feel important. This is a good thing, especially for people who consider you a friend, partner, neighbor, or associate.

Friendship is a two-way street. It's not always just about you. Just as you like to talk about things that are important to you, other people like to talk about their ideas, also. Sometimes, when you run into someone who seems to be having a bad day, why not take out time to listen to them? Instead of talking about yourself, why not hear them out, allow them to vent, and try to cheer them up for a couple of minutes. Ask questions, let them talk. That may be all they need to feel better, and you might even learn a thing or two.

Sometimes, people are longing for someone to talk to. Effective listening is a gift that many people do not have, so it's critical to be one of those who possess it. It requires taking the backseat and allowing someone else to take center stage. Let them feel significant, because you never can tell what they're going through. On another note, if you are having a bad day, you can often get your mind off your problems by listening to someone else's problems. It could give you that momentary distraction you need to manage your own stress better.

Life is so subjective. Some people sometimes feel like they have enough of something that makes them happy, so they start giving the rest away. Others can never get enough of anything. Some people will only feel rich if they have a million in the bank, whereas others always feel rich, even if they only have a grand. It's a crazy world, but as the saying goes, you will never see a Brinks (money) truck following a hearse. Whatever wealth you accumulate here doesn't follow you to the afterlife.

The lesson is to always strive to be a generous person, both with your time and your money. Try to be like a good puppy who wags more, and barks less. Learn to give without wanting anything back. I know that it's in human nature to want something back, but strive to give that nature a backseat, and cultivate a new and genuinely generous nature in its place.

Whenever you interact with another human, you should give them a gift. It doesn't have to be something physical, it could simply be wishing them well, blessing them, saying thank you, or giving a nice compliment. All of these little things could go a long way to make someone's day beautiful. Now check out the song "I, Me, Mine" by The Beatles.

Memories of Exit 11

- Get the focus off yourself and allow someone else to take the spotlight.
- Be generous with both your time and money—especially your time.
- Everyone is focused on themselves, (me, myself, and I). Focus a little more on letting someone else take center stage, and making them feel more important. That's what love is all about.

EXIT 11A

I "SEA FOOD", I EAT IT

One of the most beautiful things about eating more fish is that it cooks very fast. You can buy any type of fish, throw it on a baking pan, put some butter and paprika on it, and it'll be baked after only ten or twelve minutes. When it is done, take it out of the oven, squeeze some fresh lemon on it, and you've made yourself a beautiful meal.

It's very easy to overcook fish, so you have to check it often. You can always decide to cook it a little more, but if you overcook it, there's no turning back. If you say you don't like eating fish, you have no idea what you're missing. Tasting a little piece of delicious mild fish like cod, flounder, or sole would change your mind. At one time, our youngest daughter Kristin was a strict vegetarian. Then she started eating a little chicken and turkey. Last year, while vacationing in Maine, she tried a piece of haddock and she liked it. Since then, she has been trying different kinds of fish, little by little, now and then.

Here are a couple fish meal ideas. I will start with a really simple one. Everyone has their version of tuna salad, but here's one with a twist. This version is not applicable to making a sandwich, as it doesn't stick together too well.

Start with a few cans of tuna in olive oil. Typically, tuna in olive oil has much more flavor. Open the can, drain the olive oil, put it in a bowl, and chop it up. Add some chopped red onion and celery and fresh lemon juice. Garnish with some sliced scallion and a bit of freshly ground pepper. It's best to eat this with a fork and some warm, crusty Italian bread. Pair it with a glass of pinot grigio, and you have a super delicious meal.

Here's another exciting tuna salad sandwich recipe I bring to work once a week. Drain and chop up two cans of tuna in olive oil. Chop a third of a sweet orange pepper, half a small red onion, a jalapeño, and half a carrot (very fine). Chop a stalk of celery, a small radish, and some apples, if you want to. Then, add some chopped almonds or walnuts. Put the ingredients together, and add a few tablespoons of Hellmann's mayo. Mix thoroughly, then make a couple sandwiches on whole grain bread. Now you have a very healthy lunch.

Do you love steamed clams? This is by far the best way to prepare them. Buy a dozen little neck clams. Up here in Saratoga, our supermarkets typically get clams from the Rhode Island, Boston, or the Long Island area. If you have a decent fish store in your area, always buy clams there instead of the big supermarkets, as they will probably be fresher. The New Jersey shore has some of the finest clams. If you are ever in an area close to the ocean, Google "Fresh Fish Store" and you will find one! They sell the freshest clams.

If you are not familiar with buying clams in your area, ask the person behind the counter when the fish came in. Tell them you are going to eat them raw, even though you're not. This way, you can ask them to smell each one individually to ensure that they're fresh. Just a quick note here—fresh clams do *not* stink. If the clams you are buying smell "fishy" even in the slightest, they are not good. Ask them also to put them in a bag with ice. When you get home, put them in the fridge and do not leave the bag sealed, as the clams are alive and need to breathe.

The finest way to steam clams is in white wine, champagne, or sparkling wine. Pour a quarter of a bottle in a pot and drink the rest. You could also reduce the quantity of alcohol and use half chicken broth. Clean up a few cloves of garlic, put them through your press, and add them to the pot. Chop up a healthy bunch of fresh parsley and add it to the pot, and a quarter stick of butter. Run the clams underwater and remove any sand, etc. Add clams to the pot, cover, and turn on heat.

Put some crusty Italian bread in the oven to warm up. After about three or four minutes, check if any clams have opened. Remove each clam with tongs as they open, and put them in a bowl. If any clams do not open after another couple minutes, discard them. Pour the remaining broth over the clams (leaving the last little bit with sand in the pot) Enjoy your clams while dunking warm Italian bread in the broth or eating it like soup with a spoon.

Here's another tip: if you have any leftover juice, you can save it for a day or two and use it for the base of a future clam chowder.

Another wonderful way to prepare clams is to make them the baked or broiled way. You start by steaming them as in the above recipe, but when they are done, and you pull them out of the pot with tongs, let them cool for a moment. Then, twist off the top shell and discard. Free the clam itself from the bottom shell with a knife and keep it in the bottom shell. Proceed to sauté a mixture of chopped sweet red pepper, crushed fresh garlic, breadcrumbs, grating cheese, a little butter, and some white wine. Mix this thoroughly and add a teaspoon of it to the top of each clam.

Put in the oven for five minutes or, better still, under the broiler for a couple minutes to brown the top. Remember to keep an eye on it so it doesn't burn. It's also nice to put a small drizzle of Frank's hot sauce on them. You can also steam clams directly on your gas grill. When they open, put some of the above mixture on them, close the grill for a couple minutes, then enjoy. Watch out though, they will be extremely hot. Here is some very heavy entertainment, YouTube "VietNam Song" by Country Joe and the Fish from the original Woodstock festival in 1969.

Memories of Exit 11A

- Eat more fish. Push the envelope and try a little piece.
- Steam some clams in white wine or champagne.
- If you do not eat sushi, try an AAC roll. It stands for Avocado, Asparagus, and Cucumber.

EXIT 12

I DRINK ALONE

Let's start with a recap of what you read a few sections ago. When traveling on an interstate, never drive next to anyone. Either overtake them and move over, or slow down and drive at a reasonable distance behind them. Some people drive faster or slower than others. In an area where the speed limit is sixty-five miles per hour, some people do seventy-five or eighty comfortably. Others, on the other hand, drive strictly at sixty-five. If you are driving next to someone in the left lane with four or five cars behind you and no one in front of you, you are blocking traffic!

Always remember the "drive alone" concept. Be deliberate about staying away from other vehicles, as this is the safest way of driving. It is quite simple: the further away from any other vehicle you are, the safer you'll be if anything dangerous happens. When you want to change lanes on an interstate, always remember the "blind spot" concept. Typically, when someone is driving next to you, and the front of their car is around the back of your front door, they are in your blind spot. You won't really see them clearly in your side mirror.

The lesson here is that you shouldn't drive in anyone's "blind spot." Never drive next to someone with the front of your car around the rear of their front door. That's their blind spot, and they won't see you in their side mirror. Thank God that many newer cars now have a little light in the side view mirror that comes on when there is a vehicle next to them.

If you ever encounter someone driving erratically, tailgating you, blocking you, or doing anything you are uncomfortable with, remove yourself from the situation by getting away from them as far as possible. Alternatively, take your legs off the gas and allow them to overtake you. Do not allow yourself to be part of a road rage situation, because in most cases, it doesn't end well.

Another problem on interstates is visibility. If I am driving a tractor trailer, I don't have a visibility problem because I am sitting five feet above everyone else. When you are driving a small car and a bigger vehicle pulls in front of you, it essentially blocks your view of the "big picture." If something unexpected happens in front of them, you can't see what's going on, and the results could be devastating. If you are following a bigger vehicle too closely and they swerve to miss some debris or a pothole, you may not see that obstacle early enough to dodge it. If they hit the debris on the road, you won't have a clue until it hits you, too, and the effect may be massive on your car.

Whenever a bigger vehicle pulls in front of you, blocking your vision, get off the gas and allow a reasonable space to form between you, so you can get a clearer view of what's going on in front of you. You have to choose where to drive. Don't follow any vehicles if you're not getting a clear view of their sides. When driving, you need time to process information quickly, so you need to have enough space. Only then can you see clearly and properly decide your best line of action, especially as you're pressed for time.

If you are driving on a three-lane interstate road, it's important to be aware of what's going on when you approach an exit or entrance ramp. If there isn't much traffic, it's best to keep up your speed and use the middle lane. If you are driving in the slow lane and the person in front of you starts "checking up" with their signal light pointing right, you have to apply the brakes, check your mirrors, signal left, and slide over to the middle lane at least a half mile before the exit. This also applies to ramps. If you are in the slow lane and the person merging onto the highway doesn't have enough brain cells to accelerate out to blend in, you have to shift to the next lane to accommodate the person.

As a smart driver, you should always anticipate these kinds of things and react correctly by moving to the center lane.

When you want to use an exit ramp, keep up your speed, point your indicator light to the right, and move right to the exit lane. Then, check up (take your leg off the gas) and take the exit. The same thing applies to getting on the highway. While still on the ramp and accelerating, pick your spot and accelerate out to blend with the traffic without making anyone switch lanes for you.

Try to be conscious and stay as far away from any variables as possible. If you are driving in the slow lane and notice that someone in front has pulled over and stopped, put on your left signal, check your mirrors, and move over to the left to give everyone a little more "safety space." This is in line with the driving laws of New York state.

In some states, the law mandates you to turn on your lights when it's raining, and when driving in construction zones.

If you ever have to stop and pull over on an interstate, I advise that you don't do it. Instead, drive for another mile, get off the highway, and pull over there. If you do have to pull over and stop on an interstate because of an emergency situation, try to pull over in an area where there is no guard rail. That way, you can get an extra four or five feet away from passing traffic and be a bit safer.

Because of my level of experience, even when driving a very low Honda Civic, I notice and react to what's going on up ahead, way before everyone else around me does. This includes people in SUVs and higher smaller trucks, who should ordinarily see farther than I do due to their height. Please be more conscious of the big picture, looking as far ahead as possible, and always scanning the area and your mirrors.

The road is a very dangerous place. A small decision may either hurt or save you. Spend more time thinking about your safety in advance, more than anything else. Try to anticipate what's going to play out so you are ready to react if you have to. Keep your eyes moving, and know who is around you. Keep checking your mirrors and stay away from big trucks. Most of them are "governed" to a highway speed of around sixty-five miles per hour. They don't have a choice, so don't expect them to go faster than that. Don't hang around them, as they're very dangerous and typically overweight.

If you pay attention, you will notice all the tire parts laying on the side of the road. In New Jersey, there is a very highly traveled truck route called "two eighty-seven." You would be amazed at the amount of tire debris on that road. If a tractor trailer blows a tire, and you are next to it, it could damage your car. Plus, it's so loud that it will scare you and may cause you to lose control. If that happens, you could either skid off the road or run into another car.

Often, I am driving an overweight tanker truck full of gasoline (a big bomb), going at sixty-five miles per hour on an interstate. I am always amazed by the morons who are driving next to me for miles. Think about it. Why would someone choose to drive next to a bomb when they could be as far away as possible? Whenever you're passing a truck going downhill on an interstate, go a little faster to stay safe. Remember to always seek solitude when on the road. Driving alone is always better than driving in a pack. Play the song "I Drink Alone," by George Thorogood and The Destroyers. Print it in the back of your mind that it's peaceful to drive alone.

Memories of Exit 12

- When driving on an interstate, always try to drive alone and attempt to stay away from other vehicles when possible.
- Do not drive behind large vehicles that block you from getting the "big picture." When driving, you need time to process information that comes from that big picture. You need more space to react, because you're pressed for time.
- Stay away from tractor trailers. They are a big, dangerous piece of equipment.

EXIT 12A

"SCAMPI"

One of my favorite meals—which I have not remembered to make lately—is shrimp scampi. It's a wonderful dish that goes perfectly on rice, pasta, or garlic bread. There are so many beautiful and tasty versions of shrimp scampi. Buy some frozen shrimps, thaw them out, clean them up (as in, take off the shells, slice the back, clean out the vein, and pat them dry) then store them in a bowl in the fridge while you make your garlic bread, pasta, or rice. You have to make your carbs before you make the shrimp because the shrimp only takes a couple minutes to prepare.

Start with half a stick of butter and a splash of olive oil in a sauté pan. Finely chop one or two shallots and add five or six cloves of garlic, finely crushed, in your press. Sauté this mixture on low heat for five to ten minutes. Turn up the heat, add the shrimp, and watch out for when they turn pink and curl. That's how you know they're done. One thing about shrimp is that they cook very fast, so it's very easy to overcook them. You do not want to overcook them, or they will turn to rubber.

Years ago, a chef friend of mine taught me a nice way of adding a different texture to shrimp scampi. Take a quarter cup of breadcrumbs and mix it in with a quarter stick of melted butter. Let it cool in the fridge for half an hour. When you are ready to serve the shrimp, fluff the breadcrumb mixture up a little bit and dust the top of the scampi. It adds a different texture!

Here's how to make the sauce. Take the shrimp out when done and put them in the oven at 200, while you make the sauce. At this point, turn up the heat in the pan, add a little chicken broth, a couple pats of butter, a good splash of white wine, some lemon juice, and a generous portion of Frank's hot sauce. Reduce the heat and let it simmer for two to three minutes. You are done! Serve the shrimp on the garlic bread, rice, or pasta, and pour over a generous amount of your sauce. You can garnish with fresh parsley, the breadcrumb mixture, and a dusting of grating cheese. Pour a nice glass of wine and enjoy. As you get more comfortable with multitasking in the kitchen, steamed asparagus with fresh lemon is a wonderful side for your scampi.

Another great version would be to add half a cup of milk or cream and a few tablespoons of good grating cheese after you sauté the shallot and garlic mixture. Toast up a few slices of rye bread, spread some butter on them, and break them up in a bowl. Add the browned shrimp and the sauce over the top. Yummy! After you get comfortable making "scampi" you can add many interesting ingredients. Lately, I have been chopping up some mushrooms, a yellow or orange bell pepper, and half a cup of Kalamata olives. I also toast some Italian bread, put the cooked shrimp on the toast, add a sliced chunk of feta, and put it in the broiler for a minute or two (feta does not melt easily).

When I take it out of the broiler and plate it up, I then pour the reduction of the oil, butter, garlic, orange pepper, mushroom, and white wine on top, add a little chopped fresh parsley, and enjoy.

Many times, when I make scampi I start with a couple pats of butter and a healthy splash of olive oil in a sauté pan. Then I start with my chopping obsession. I start with a small amount of finely chopped carrot, orange, or yellow pepper, and maybe a jalapeño. I also chop some shallots, mushrooms, and fresh spinach. Not only that, but I also add a splash of chicken broth and white wine. Sauté this mixture on low heat for fifteen minutes, adding the liquid of your choice as it reduces. At this time, throw in eight to ten shrimps, sauté for three to four minutes, and you have an exciting meal.

If you want to add a twist to the above recipe, right before you add the shrimp, you could add half a cup of heavy cream, half a can of crushed Italian tomatoes, and tons of grating cheese. Add them little by little, then you add the shrimp and sauté for a couple minutes. That's all! Serve over warm Italian bread, rice, pasta, or the grain of your choice. Quinoa, anyone? Another version involves not adding the shrimp. Cook the shrimp separately in a very hot pan with just a little olive oil and butter. Let the shrimp brown in the hot pan, and dish it into a plate. Then, pour the sauce over the shrimp! This version gives you a little crunch.

You could also make any of the above sauces and pour it over scallops. An easy way to have scallops come out perfectly is to dry them first, then roll them around in flour and proceed to fry them in butter until they turn brown a little. When you put your scallops in the oiled and buttered pan, do not move them until you see a little brown on the edge. You can check how to make a "Beurre Blanc" sauce on YouTube for more inspiration.

Just today, I toasted some Italian bread in the broiler, added some sautéed spinach with the excess water squeezed out, crumbled feta, browned shrimp, and added a coating of good grating cheese. I put the covered bread back in the broiler for five to seven minutes, and afterward, I had myself a delicious meal.

While you prepare to make any of these meals, I'd like you to listen to "Highwayman" by the Highwaymen (Johnny Cash, Waylon Jennings, Kris Kristofferson, and Willie Nelson).

Memories of Exit 12A

- Start honing your shrimp scampi skills. Experiment with a bunch of different versions and ingredients.
- Remember that shrimp cooks very fast and they are very easy to overcook.

EXIT 13

I AIN'T SUPERSTITIOUS.

Since time immemorial, superstitious beliefs have been an undeniable part of human nature. People still skip the thirteenth floor when numbering tall buildings, and instead, name it the fourteenth floor. Well, unlike them, I'm not superstitious, so I'm not skipping over Exit Thirteen!

Why do people think thirteen is an unlucky number? This is something that has been going on for a long time. There are even references that trace it back to the Last Supper. Personally, I don't think that thirteen is an unlucky number, but I've heard people say, "I'd rather be lucky than good." Well, in this exit, we are going to make the number thirteen lucky. You may ask how? Well, we will do it by simply deciding to. Remember what Henry Ford said: you can believe you can, or believe you can't, either way you're right.

It's time for a mental shift. Grab your mind's remote, point it at your brain, and say, "From now on, the number thirteen is a lucky number in my life." I love going against the grain. Imagine being able to turn a bad luck thing into good luck just by using your brain. As an author, I've declared this exit thirteen a lucky exit. If you don't feel lucky enough to beat thirteen, I'll give you some reasons to reassess your feelings.

Firstly, life is a gamble, and you're still in the game. So, in essence, you're lucky because you are still alive. Many people out there have lost their minds and can't articulate their thoughts, but you're coherent because you're reading this. Your mind can process all the information you've read so far. You probably can smile, love, think, dream, walk, talk, drive, eat, drink, and wipe your you-know-what. That's being lucky. Not everyone has all that "luxury."

When you are young, you take a lot of things for granted. You're in a zone where you think you are going to live forever. But as you get older, you start thinking about how much time you have left to live. You start to appreciate things a little more, things that didn't mean much to you when you were young. At some point, you get to realize the small things that you take for granted are really the big things. You start to realize that it's very easy to get caught up in bullshit that really doesn't matter.

If you are in a casino, you are hoping for some good luck—but most of the time, success comes from hard and smart work. It doesn't often happen magically by winning a jackpot. This doesn't mean jackpots don't happen. People get lucky sometimes.

We all know that we can build muscle through regular exercise. But is there something we can do to build our ability to have more good luck? I think there is. You just need to exercise the "lucky part of your brain" by viewing things differently.

Life is really about what you choose to believe. Remember that the only way to help yourself is to help someone else, so start by doing something special for someone. You know, something that makes someone feel lucky. Buy your partner flowers, buy a co-worker a cup of coffee, pick up the tab if you can afford it, tell someone you appreciate them. There are endless ways to be extra nice or appreciative to someone. I think one of the best ways to get lucky is to do a good deed that no one knows about, and not brag about it later. If no one knows about your good deed, and you don't tell anyone, it doesn't appeal to your ego. It's simply a good thing for the universe and humankind. If you can practice this concept, you'll realize that you can get happiness by spreading happiness. Don't forget, what goes around, comes around. Don't be that guy who throws their gum in the urinal. Karma will catch up with you instantly.

To close Exit Thirteen, here's some very important information to go over. If you want to be lucky, you have to have an open mind and save some room for learning. You have to be in control of your brain and mind, because they're the tools you will use to create the "outline" for a better life. If you take the time to read all this information and do not put any of it into practice, then you've successfully wasted your time, and clearly don't know how to learn.

Try some of the things you've read so far. Use them to make some changes and improvements to your life—after all, you are a work in progress. To do the same thing over and over and expect to get different results is insanity. As hockey great Wayne Gretzky said, you miss 100 percent of the shots you don't take. Take a shot at spreading happiness and good luck. Cultivate the habit of saying, "It's all good." Learn to use these words 'til they become true for you. If you're unhappy for some reason, change your goals. Laugh at yourself once in a while, and as I mentioned before, wag more and bark less.

You lucky person! Listen to the song by Stevie Wonder "Superstition."

Memories of Exit 13

- The number thirteen can be a lucky number if you want it to be. Reconfigure your mind and believe that it's your lucky number.
- My lucky number is 17. "Q" is the seventeenth letter in the alphabet. (One of our grand daughters is named Quinn)
- You don't have to keep waiting to feel lucky. You can create that lucky feeling by doing things that make others feel lucky.
- Don't wait for the future. Create it now. "The longer you wait for the future, the shorter it will be"

EXIT 13A

WHICH CAME FIRST, THE...

Eggs are a superfood. They're loaded with all kinds of nutrients our bodies need. The other day, I noticed a larger-than-normal crowd coming out of a Dunkin' Donuts. I kind of felt bad for them. Everyone was walking out with their bags of carbs and chemicals, and heading out to wherever. Believe me, I love their coffee, but I am not a donut or junk bagel kind of guy. I am from New Jersey, so I know what a real bagel is. Instead of going to Dunkin' Donuts, you would be better off boiling a dozen eggs and taking them to work. That's way better than a freaking donut. Hard-boiled eggs are pretty easy to carry around in your lunch cooler. You can even add some fun twists by preparing "deviled eggs."

There are so many ways to prepare eggs, but when you are home, this method for scrambled eggs is the simplest and the most delicious, especially if you like them "loose." I heard that it's called the French method of making scrambled eggs. There are only two ingredients: eggs and butter, with maybe a little salt and pepper.

Start by melting a couple pats of butter in a nonstick pan. Crack two or three eggs directly into the pan. The big secret here is to never stop moving the eggs until you turn them onto a plate. As soon as you break the eggs into the pan, start scrambling them with your plastic spatula, constantly scraping the bottom of the pan and moving the mixture on medium to low heat. In some cases, you may even need to take the pan on and off the heat as you make this beautiful mixture. When the eggs reach your desired loose consistency, add a bit of salt and pepper, then you dish them out and enjoy.

The next egg recipe is called a Frittata. For this recipe, you need a well-seasoned cast iron pan or a nonstick skillet that has no plastic on it. This is because you'll finish this dish in the broiler. Begin by chopping a small amount of sweet red, orange, or yellow pepper. Add a quarter of a chopped-up, cooked squash or zucchini. Add a chopped jalapeño, chopped red onion, and two or three finely pressed garlic cloves. Next, add either chopped pre-cooked sausage, bacon, or some quarter-inch chunks of ham. You can then add some nicely chopped fresh parsley and six to eight eggs. Scramble them all up in a big bowl, and set aside.

Heat up a non-stick pan, melt a few pats of butter in it, and add the mixture. Start cooking it on low heat, moving the pan around on the stove a little so it cooks evenly. Just like in the previous recipe, you may take the pot off the heat occasionally so it doesn't burn the bottom. After about seven to eight minutes, cut up thin pieces of sharp cheddar and add them all around the top. Finish it in the broiler.

Please keep an eye on it if you are not familiar with broiling. In the end, dish it on a plate, cut it open as if it was a pie, and splash some

Frank's hot sauce on it. There are many other ingredients you could add to this frittata to make it interesting—shallots, other types of peppers, spinach, finely chopped carrots, fresh tomatoes, etc.

I saw another exciting egg recipe in *Cook's Magazine* a couple years ago. To make it, you need a large onion and a large red pepper. Slice both of them sideways, then pick out one big and thin circular ring from each. Put this onion ring in a frying pan, and add the pepper ring either inside or outside the onion. Break an egg and fry it with this ring holding it together. When it's done, you can add a slice of cheddar and finish it in the broiler.

I love frying some bacon and cooking up a couple of sunny side up eggs in the remaining bacon fat. You simply tip the pan and spoon the bacon fat over the sunny side up egg to cook the top a little.

When making Caesar salad, I always use a raw egg yolk in the dressing. Let me share the recipe, but bear in mind that it's more fun if you have a wooden bowl. Start by mashing some cloves of garlic in a bowl. If you have anchovies, add two or three. If you don't have any, don't worry about it. Crack an egg above another bowl and separate the yolk from the white. Scoop out the egg yolk and add it to the garlic mixture. Add some squirts of Worcestershire sauce, half a teaspoon of mustard (Maille), and start mixing, while adding olive oil a little at a time. At this point, start adding my fave—Parmigiano-Reggiano—the greatest cheese in the world. Mix all these ingredients and add one-and-half-inch ripped or cut pieces of Romaine lettuce. Mix thoroughly to completely coat the lettuce, and add an extra dusting of cheese when serving. This is one of the most amazing dishes in the world.

Another interesting breakfast egg recipe is to separate the whites from the yolk, make a meringue with the whites (whip them with an electric beater), then gently fold in the yolks. Pour this in a sauté pan and cook on very low heat for a couple of minutes. After that, put it in an oven for a few minutes. This approach gives you a really fluffy egg dish. Listen to the Eagles song by Glenn Frey, "The Heat is On."

Memories of Exit 13A

- Eggs are a super food with many versatile recipes. Get creative and start cooking them instead of stuffing your system with donuts.
- You can YouTube how to make a beautiful quiche for dinner and have leftovers for breakfast.
- A hard boiled egg is better for you than junk food.

EXIT 14

"I'M IN A HURRY TO GET THINGS DONE, OH, I RUSH AND RUSH UNTIL LIFE'S NO FUN!"

Alabama

Think about the different "styles" of driving. Let's look at the two extremes:

A) You are on your way to somewhere very important; you are late and stressed out, driving fast and super aggressive because you are in such a hurry.
B) You are taking a scenic drive in the country with a good friend or your lover, relaxing and just looking at all the pretty scenery.

These would be the two opposite ends of the spectrum. Whatever style you are presently involved in, it's critical to have some respect for drivers on the other end of the spectrum. If you are on a two-lane rural road driving slowly, and someone who is in a hurry is tailgating you, courtesy demands that you put on your right signal, slow down and pull over briefly, to let them pass. If you were on the other end, being the tailgater in a hurry, you would appreciate it if the person in front of you lets you pass.

I believe that most of the time, driving is so automatic, that people don't put much thought into being courteous. But then, imagine if that one little act of courtesy could save someone's life or save them from many other problems. Imagine if they're rushing to meet up with an urgent, life-changing business deal. In hindsight, if you ever get to know their ordeal, you'd wish you let them pass.

As the saying goes, hindsight is 20/20. Right now, it's not too late to learn how to make better driving decisions. Be helpful to other drivers, even when they upset you. I think we should all offer a little more common courtesy on the road. Let's face it, all the annoying stuff you accuse other drivers of doing? You've also been guilty of doing the same things at one time or another.

Just the other day on the Adirondack Northway, I thought I was moving at a pretty decent pace of about eighty miles per hour. But suddenly, six or eight cars zoomed past me moving at over ninety. One of the things that make people drive like that is ego. They want to prove to you that their car is better than yours, they're a better driver than you, or they're faster than you. This "I am better than you" mindset can create a lot of problems on the road.

Let's face it, it's fun to drive fast. Too many people drive aggressively because they want to have fun, or they think they are "cool." But being too aggressive on the road is quite dangerous, and is not a very smart way to be cool. It's one thing to get into an accident because it was truly an accident, but it's another thing to get into an accident because you are driving like a jerk, thinking you're cool.

I believe the world is in too much of a hurry. Every day, we all should consciously make efforts to slow down and smell the roses. This doesn't only apply to driving but to eating and living, generally. Take a deep breath, look around you, and think about a couple of good things you have going on for you. When you have the time—and guess what? You always do—I want you to start wrapping your mind around being smooth and gentle. You should consider turning the wheels a little more gently, hitting the gas gently, and matching the brakes gently. When you interact with other people, be considerate of their feelings.

On the subject of being smooth and gentle, the other day I was driving with someone on the interstate and I noticed they kept turning the wheel this way and that repeatedly. I tried to explain to them to aim the wheel straight and keep it steady in one position. I told them to adjust the steering wheel so they can control it with their fingers, palm up, resting on their leg. They tried it, and got the hang of it. But within a couple minutes, they went back to their old style of placing their hands at ten and two, moving back and forth constantly. As I said, driving is all about habits. I have another friend who cannot keep one steady pressure on the gas pedal; they are constantly stepping on the gas pedal, withdrawing their leg, stepping on it again, and withdrawing again. I feel my body weight going back and forth whenever I ride with them. That's not how to drive! Be smooth. Keep your foot in one position, and only change it when it's absolutely necessary.

YouTube the Eddie Rabbit song, "Drivin' My Life Away."

Memories of Exit 14

- Remember the two different driving scenarios in the beginning of this exit, and have respect for others.
- Try to "slow down" your life. Slow down when you're eating, slow down when you are driving, and think about being a little smoother overall. Chill out and enjoy this wonderful life. Stop and smell the roses.

EXIT 14A

SLAUGHTER THE SLAW

We have already hammered on the importance of eating foods with more water. You also already know that the best way to set yourself up for success is to always make soups. Here's another option. You can buy different colored peppers and a container of hummus. Cut up the pepper, a carrot, a cucumber, dip it in the hummus, and eat. It's delicious, and you'd be getting lots of water. Personally, I use different flavored hummus on sandwiches instead of mayonnaise.

Chop up those veggies in a container and leave it in front of the half-and-half or milk you use in your morning coffee. The next morning, put it in your cooler and take it to work. During the day, you can nibble on veggies instead of eating garbage. Another healthy option is to snack on some celery stuffed with peanut butter or cream cheese and chopped green olives with a paprika garnish. What about some fresh blackberries, strawberries, and blueberries. You can also buy some grapes, and while preparing it the night before, add some shelled walnuts or a couple almonds. These will give you water, fiber, and tons of nutrients. They're many times better than donuts, processed bread, cake, or styrofoam-like carbs.

Some days ago, I bought a cute little head of cabbage. I have big plans to make a small batch of coleslaw with it. Coleslaw is actually quite simple, loaded with fiber, vitamins, and minerals. It's one of my favorites to bring for lunch. Buy some pre-packaged coleslaw mix. It typically has some chopped carrots in it already, but you can decide to chop more carrots and add to it as you chop your cabbage. Next, add some horseradish to taste. Put a healthy amount of mayonnaise and a few squirts of agave (or chopped apple). Mix thoroughly, then add salt and white pepper to taste.

You can choose to skip the mayo and use a mixture of oil and vinegar instead. Coleslaw is very good for you. Some people argue that there is too much fat in the mayonnaise, but think about this: eating plenty of vegetables with some fat is still better than not eating a vegetable. Always use white pepper, and Celtic sea salt, as that really makes a "slaw." On another note, I like my slaw chopped very fine, whereas my wife hates it that way. Well, variety is what makes the world go round. Here's another great recipe for a healthy garnish:Clean up a few jalapeños (take out the seeds and the white part). Chop them up, add some chopped red onion, squeeze some fresh lemon or lime, add some chopped-up cilantro and chopped mango, pineapple, or some other sweet fruit. Put it all in a container, mix, and put it in the fridge for a couple of hours. You would be amazed at how delicious it turns out.

What about salad dressing? Here is my favorite recipe:

Get three tablespoons of extra virgin olive oil, two tablespoons of red wine vinegar or lemon, and one tablespoon of Dijon mustard. Add a tablespoon of water and a splash of agave. Put all these ingredients in a container, shake to mix thoroughly. You may also choose to add a little bit of finely-crushed garlic.

Hey, thinking of "slaw" again, guess what rhymes with "slaw?" Mother-in-law. There's an old song from the sixties by Ernie K-Doe titled, "Mother-in-Law." Check it out.

Memories of Exit 14A

- Make and eat more coleslaw.
- If you say you do not like coleslaw, try adding some agave to it. This might change your beliefs.

EXIT 15

CALL THE "WHAAAMBULANCE."

The more you do something, the more you get used to it. With time, it becomes "normal" to you. Normal means something we expect to happen, so we don't raise an eyebrow when it does. Normal means different things to different people, so what I consider normal may seem insane to you.If you are in the habit of complaining, odds are you are going to have an unhappy life because you spend large amounts of time focusing on how bad your problems are. For you, it's the normal thing to do. If you are in the habit of blaming someone else for problems in your life, odds are you are going to have an unhappy life, and you'll feel it's their fault that your life is so bad.

If you are constantly crying, "whaaa whaaa whaaa," so it sounds like someone needs to call the "whaaambulance," then you should get in touch with me. I will mail you a box of tissues. Maybe I could start a company and call it "Tissues for Issues," with labels on the tissue boxes like, "broke," "in debt," "divorced," or "not appreciated." Okay, that's a joke; but seriously, why are you so focused on your problems? Why not focus on being thankful for all the good things you have going on in your life? If you get in the habit of being thankful for every good thing going on for you, no matter how small or insignificant, you will probably be a pretty happy camper. If you're often conscious of the fact that the things you do every day bring you and your loved ones closer to living a better life, you probably feel confident that you are a work in progress and your future is bright. It's quite simple. Think about your habits. Are you a happy person or a complainer?

It amazes me that so many people who we interact with on a daily basis spend all their time crying about their problems. That's all they think about, constantly. Think about your habits and think about steps you can take to change so you can improve your life and that of the people around you. Remember, it's all small habits that add up to giving you a wonderful or miserable life. Once a day, say, "God (if you're not a believer, say, "Universe"), please send me your infinite wisdom. Teach me to have a peaceful, prosperous, and loving day." After saying this, you can then have a drink and celebrate life. If you spend an hour a day working on a subject, in five years, you could be a national expert. Just think, if you work on being happy daily, in a couple of years, you could be a "happiness expert."

Every day, grab your "remote" and change your brain to the happy channel. What do you want to become an expert in? Like what Morgan Freeman said in *The Shawshank Redemption,* "Either get busy living or get busy dying."

Memories of Exit 15

- Stop crying about your problems and be thankful for the little things you have working out for you.

EXIT 15A

BASIC ONION SOUP

I think onion soup is one of the greatest foods to eat. There are so many versions, but the key to making a delicious one is to always keep it simple. The one thing you will need in the beginning of this recipe is time—it takes a good forty-five minutes to brown (or caramelize) the onions, and you have to pay constant attention to it. You need onions, oil, butter, chicken or beef broth (I prefer beef), red wine, some grating cheese, a teaspoon of Dijon mustard, a splash of A1 Steak Sauce, and maybe some sliced fresh scallions for a garnish. You can also add a piece of toast and a bit of white wine for deglazing. You need a big frying pan, preferably not non-stick, because you want the sugar from the onions to caramelize on the pan (which you will deglaze with broth or wine).

Melt a generous amount of butter and a heavy splash of olive oil in a frying pan. Add five or six properly sliced, large, sweet yellow onions. (Bonus tip: they say if you breathe through your mouth while you are chopping onions, you will cry less.) Using a spatula, start moving the onions around the pan. As they start cooking, after fifteen or twenty minutes, you will notice that the onions have started to turn a little brown here and there. This is what you are looking for. Continue stirring, and the color change will become more apparent. This is the "caramelizing" process. The longer you can keep this happening, the better. The onions will get darker and darker as you keep stirring. Make sure you keep the heat low enough that you do not burn them.

Now add a cup of water. As that dissipates in the mixture, it will get a little darker. Add a little more water and repeat. At this point, deglaze the pan by adding a good splash of white wine or broth. Use your spatula to scrape the "fond" forming on the bottom of the pan. Keep scraping and stirring for another ten minutes. While at it, continue adding tiny amounts of liquid until everything turns a medium to dark color.When you get the desired color, your work is almost done. Add the mixture to a decent-sized pot, then scrape up all the fond in the original pan by adding liquid to loosen it. Add a box of chicken or beef broth, a half cup of red wine, and a couple cloves of garlic run through the press. Put in the other ingredients I mentioned above and let the mixture simmer for an hour or two.

You can also add a splash of soy sauce and Worcestershire. For some reason, just like most foods, this soup gets better the next day. There are many variants of this onion soup, but what I just shared is the basic recipe. It's all about taking the time to "caramelize" the onions. You can vary the remaining process as you like. In the end, garnish with some Gruyere, toast, or anything else you like. I like to garnish mine with a little chopped scallions. Remember, you can make this soup as rich as you want just by cooking it more, which reduces it and makes it richer. If you are going to reduce it quite a bit, I would recommend using a "low sodium" broth or stock.

Try this sometime: start with a huge batch and try cooking it all day. You'll be amazed at the richness. If you have the correct oven proof bowls, you could add cheese to the top and throw them in the broiler for a couple minutes. Of course, always remember to keep an eye on them.

Everyone has a different hobby. One of our latest obsessions is trying onion soup at different places. Recently, we tried it at a popular restaurant, and it was one of the worst versions we've ever had. When they served it, it looked pretty good—the color was very dark, it had a nice melted rim of cheese-but guess what? It had zero taste. I mean, it tasted like dishwater. This happened at a really popular place. But then, remember that everyone can have a bad day, even a chef. While you are crying from chopping onions, you should listen to "Crying" by Roy Orbison.

Memories of Exit 15A

- How long are you going to wait until you make some beautiful, homemade onion soup?

EXIT 16

SKIP THIS EXIT IF YOU DON'T PLAN ON KEEPING YOUR CAR FOR MORE THAN A *HUNERT* THOUSAND!!!

Your car's motor needs to be lubricated to keep running efficiently. That's why you have oil constantly circulating through your motor. Gasoline is the opposite of a lubricant. If you live in an area that has a cold winter, and you start your vehicle quite often at a below-freezing temperature, here's some information you need to know.

To start a gasoline engine in the winter, the initial gas-to-air ratio has to be richer for a quick cold start. Nowadays, because of electronic fuel injection, it all happens automatically. What this means is that when you first start your car during cold weather, the gas-to-air mixture is very rich. And remember, gasoline is a cleaner, not a lubricant. So at colder temperatures, the "rich" gas-to-air mixture kind of "cleans" the cylinder walls of the oil lubricant. There is also the condensation factor, where cold metal could accumulate little water beads which also hurts the lubricating factor at start up—and decreases oil life. Simple fix: whenever you start your vehicle during the cold weather, don't turn it off until it is fully warmed up (heat is coming out of the heater). If you often drive short distances during the winter, I would advise you to change your oil regularly—like, every two months—disregarding mileage.

I have had quite a few vehicles that reached over 250,000 miles, including a 2004 Honda Civic with 253,000 miles (it did ninety miles per hour on a daily basis), and a 2003 Toyota Avalon with 272,000. Altogether, both cars have covered the earth sixteen times. There's also a 2004 Chevy Silverado I sold to my son-in-law, with 220,000 mileage. He ran it up to 400,000 with no major motor work. I bring this up because whenever you eat French fries, you can tell if the oil is old or burnt. Just like your mouth, your engine also has taste buds. If you want to keep your cars as long as I do, fresh oil is very important.

On another note: if you live in an area where they use salt on the roads in the winter, rust can pose a big issue. If you use your vehicle every day, it will not rust out as fast as a car that sits for a couple days without moving around. If you wear glasses, you probably understand how condensation works. When you walk into a warm room after staying outside in the cold, your glasses steam up because of condensation. The same thing happens to the metal on your vehicle. At night, the metal gets cold, but when the sun rises, and it warms up, little beads of water will appear on the car. Underneath, if it is not driven, it stays wet for longer. This leads to premature rust.

Another factor to consider is where the car parks on a daily basis. If the car is parked on dirt, gravel, or grass, the underneath will stay wet because of moisture coming out of the earth. But if it's parked on a blacktop or concrete where the moisture does not come up, it will not stay as wet for as long. Based on where you live, there are things you need to consider to avoid damage to your car. Because of technological advances, vehicles last much longer now than they did thirty years ago. In the old days, a set of spark plugs would never last 100,000 miles; now it's pretty common to see them lasting so long. All the things mentioned in this exit are very critical if you plan on keeping your vehicle for a long time—which is a good idea. Because of inflation, government safety laws, technological advances, creature comforts, and energy costs, automobiles are very expensive and their second-hand value depreciates fast.If you plan on keeping your vehicle for many years, *and* want to drive for hundreds of thousands of miles, I would advise you to stay away from a motor with a turbo charger. Cars with turbochargers typically have a smaller motor with more power because the turbo charger compresses more air and fuel into the motor—and hence, has more power. It's great for a high-performance machine, but because of extra stress, it has less longevity.

My first new car in 1970 cost $1,800. Now, a comparable new car would cost about $25,000 to $30,000. Our daughter was looking to buy a new 2024 Chevy Tahoe—wow, over $50,000! Cars cost so much nowadays, so you can save a lot of money (and invest it) by maintaining your car a little better and keeping it for longer. Always remember that there are only two things you can do with money: spend it or invest it. Saving money is the same as spending it, because inflation will eat it away. A grand does not buy what it would have bought even five years ago. To end this exit, I'd like you to check out Sammy Hagar's song, "I Can't Drive 55."

Memories of Exit 16

- If you plan on keeping your vehicle for over 100,000 miles, remember to always use synthetic oil.
- Check all your fluids constantly, especially your coolant level.
- Always look for leaks, and check your tires' air pressure regularly.

EXIT 16A

SARATOGA SALAD (I MADE UP THE NAME)

Always remember, if you want to live longer, eat more plants. Here's how to make Saratoga Salad: I like to start every salad with baby spinach, some thinly sliced cucumber, a few thin slices of radish, and a couple pieces of chopped celery. I also add some chopped red onion, a little finely chopped carrot, a few slices of red, orange, or yellow peppers, a couple sliced mushrooms, a few chopped green or black olives, or maybe some Kalamata olives. And then there's some crumbled up feta or cheddar, a few Mezzetta tamed jalapeño slices (from a jar), maybe some crumbled bacon, and a few chopped walnuts. I don't leave out a couple avocado slices, a sliced hard-boiled egg, chopped watermelon or strawberries, and sliced artichoke hearts. The list goes on and on.

At the time of writing this exit, it was zucchini and eggplant season up here in Saratoga. One day, while Deb was sautéing some chopped-up zucchini and eggplant, I got an idea on how to add a little twist to the said preparation above. I drained all the liquid, placed it in a shallow baking dish, added a thin layer of breadcrumbs, threw on five slices of cheddar, a generous dusting of Romano grating cheese, and a garnish of fresh parsley. Then, I proceeded to brown it in the broiler. I have to say, it was incredible.

After preparing the salad, here's another way we make our homemade salad dressing: You'll need soy sauce, a freshly squeezed lemon, one or two finely pressed cloves of garlic, a tiny amount of sesame oil, a squirt of olive oil, and a splash of agave. Mix them together, and you'll have a yummy dressing for your salad. (Maybe add a little Dijon mustard, too.)

These next two recipes are straight out of one of my favorite cookbooks, *My Beverly Hills Kitchen* by Alex Hits. They are not really salsas, but they can be used as such. We will start with broccoli puree. As Alex states, sometimes the simplest recipes become magnificent. Bring two quarts of water to boil, add a tablespoon of salt, drop in two pounds of broccoli, and boil for about five minutes. Remove from heat and drain in a colander.

In a food processor or blender, purée the broccoli in batches until it is smooth (forget the blender or food processor—use an immersion blender). Transfer it to a medium mixing bowl and add a quarter cup of heavy cream and a teaspoon of salt. Stir it well and serve. The carrot purée is essentially the same, except that you must boil two pounds of carrots for twelve minutes and forget the cream. Add half a stick of butter and two tablespoons of freshly grated ginger. According to Alex, carrot purée with ginger and broccoli are excellent together, and they look gorgeous too.

Talking about Saratoga, listen to the song by Carly Simon "You're So Vain."

Memories of Exit 16A

- I said it before, but it is worth repeating: don't just read about these recipes, try them.
- Remember what the author Dan Buettner wrote in *Blue Zones*: "Want to live longer? Eat more veggies."

EXIT 17

DREAM, DREAM, DREAM

What are your life's dreams and ambitions? Do you know? If you don't know now, you better get busy figuring it out. They say if you find your true calling, you will never work a day in your life. Is it really true? I have been lucky in many areas of my life, so I'm not complaining. But there is an excitement and fulfillment that comes with doing things you truly love.

What do you love doing? If you are presently doing what you love, consider yourself blessed. If you don't, why not try to spend a little time each day working toward getting your dream job or business? As Steve Jobs would say, once you find it, your life will just keep getting better and better. But before then, you need to always remember that everything starts with a dream.

Some years ago, when I was really young, I was able to climb up high framing houses pretty fast. Although I can't pull off those stunts now, when I look at what I accomplished when I was stronger, I get an awesome feeling. Going from a farm field to a framed-up house, weathered in with (shingles on, windows in) within two weeks made me feel so good. Framing different, complicated dormers and all kinds of complicated hips and valleys was all fun, too. At some point, putting all those things in place was my dream, but just like everything else, dreams change. Those are no longer my dreams because I have surpassed them.

It's okay to get new dreams, new goals and new visions each time it seems like you're done with the former. If, for any reason, you don't know what your "true calling" is, just keep trying to do as many things as you can until you find your actual purpose. As Charles Darwin said, it's not the strongest of the species that survive, nor the most intelligent. It is one that is most responsive to change. If you want to survive, you have to embrace change. (Note how many times I have subtly hinted at this.)

I am no longer interested in fast cars. When I was younger, I used to be obsessed with them. I hated to get rid of our 2019 Civic Sport for an HRV back in 2021, but the Civic was getting a little harder to get in and out of as we got older. Now, we prioritize comfort!

When I was young, I didn't care about football, but now I love it. If you told me ten years ago that I would be into cooking, growing flowers and vegetables, and writing a book, I would have told you, no way! If we were to hit the lottery, my wife and I would travel a little, but our big goal would be to buy solar panels and to heat our greenhouse—which we could afford to build—so we could grow plants all year-round up here in the north country. I would even love to learn more about hydroponic growing.

The lesson here is that whatever it is that you want to do, don't push it out so far into the future. Don't say, "Someday I'm going to do this or that." Instead, add a definite date to it. Say something like, "On Monday, the sixth of April, I am going to do this or that." Guess what? There is no "someday" on a calendar. Pick a real day to do something that you dream about doing.

Did you know that "interests" are what keeps you happy in life? When you are preoccupied with something you enjoy, you tend to lose track of time. When you are in "that zone" when your creative juice is at its peak, you forget that you're in a hurry and just want to stick to what you're doing until you're done.

Lately, I've been hearing the term "bucket list." Do you have a written bucket list? What's on it? If you don't, maybe you should spend some time thinking about a list of the things you want to do in your life. I think we all should be spending a little more time dreaming about fun stuff instead of things that stress us out.

Here's one of the things on my bucket list for this summer: Deborah and I are going to take the five-hour cruise all the way up Lake George. Starting from the million-dollar beach in the village, we'll sail thirty-three miles all the way up to Ticonderoga. The tour boat goes through an area called "the Narrows," which is quite picturesque! We have taken quite a few shorter cruises in the lower area of Lake George, and we have been up maybe ten miles—as far as The Sagamore in Bolton Landing—but we have never been all the way up to Ticonderoga on a cruise boat.

I would love to see "Highway to the Sun" in Glacier National Park. I would love to travel around Prince Edward Island some summer. I would love to get out of the winter for a week and go to an all-inclusive resort in the Caribbean. I have some bigger dreams on my bucket list, but the most important one is the dream of finishing this book. I will never stop dreaming, and I will be adding things to my bucket list as long as I live. The license plate on our car says "UDREAMN." I think you should adopt the same mindset. Take a moment to update your bucket list for the next couple of months, and start working on making them happen, because no one will live forever.

Check out the song "All I Have to Do is Dream" by The Everly Brothers.

Memories of Exit 17

- Everything begins with a dream, if you are going to dream, you may as well dream big.
- There is no "someday" on a calendar. Plan on working toward something that brings you closer to actualizing your dream, and put a real date on it.
- Remember, those who love the journey are typically happier than those who love the destination.

EXIT 17A

A COUPLE "GO-TOS"

How about some sliders? Start by chopping up some shallots and jalapeño peppers. Fry them in some butter or olive oil with a healthy splash of agave at the end. Make two small hamburgers and plop them into the shallot mixture, flip them over, and add a couple thin slices of cheddar. Put them on a few pieces of semolina Italian bread, add a generous splash of Frank's hot sauce, crack a couple of Miller Lites, and enjoy.

How about some Italian red sauce with sausage and little neck clams over angel hair pasta? Here's a simple recipe:

Scrub the clams clean before starting. I like steaming clams in white wine and garlic—I would say a cup of white wine and three or four cloves per dozen clams. Keep an eye on them and take them out of the pot with tongs as soon as they open. Then, put them in a separate bowl. Pour the remaining liquid into a different pot, leaving the sand in the original pot to discard. In the new pot, add a can of crushed tomatoes and some chopped veggies of your choice. Cook for a half hour. In a frying pan, cut up the sausage and fry them till they turn brown. When the sausage is done, add it to the sauce and also add a half cup of red wine.

Start making your pasta in a pot of salted water. When your pasta is done, drain it, add the clams to your sauce, and dish it out. Get some good grating cheese and a bottle of white wine, and enjoy. You can also pair it with a little garlic bread.Another of our favorites is a vodka sauce. Start by sautéing a large quantity of finely chopped onion in a stick of butter for about twenty minutes on low heat. Add a cup of vodka and a can of crushed tomatoes, then sauté for another twenty minutes. Add a half cup of heavy cream and a half cup of good grating cheese, then sauté for about another ten minutes. (I'm repeating this recipe on purpose, because it's yummy.)

Cook some pasta, dish it out, and add a healthy amount of grating cheese and freshly ground black pepper. Pour a nice wine of your choice, grab the chunk of bread out of the oven, put a touch of garlic butter on it, and enjoy. Sometimes I garnish this with a couple sliced scallions.

Here is a wonderful recipe from our friend Michelle at McGregor Pub in Wilton. It is a dipping sauce for asparagus, but it has many uses. Take a half cup of mayonnaise, add a few tablespoons of chopped capers, add two or three cloves of crushed fresh garlic, chop five or six sprigs of fresh parsley, and add some squeezes of fresh lemon. Mix thoroughly and enjoy. How about some Simon and Garfunkel, "Parsley, Sage, Rosemary, and Thyme."

Memories of Exit 17A

- The sliders fried on top of the shallot, jalapeño, agave mixture are to die for!
- The mayo, capers, and garlic dip is breathtaking.
- We love the Vodka sauce.

EXIT 18

BLINDED BY THE LIGHT OR BLINDED BY LACK OF LIGHT?

As time changes, so does visibility. Dusk is the hardest time to see, because your eyes do not adjust as quickly to the changing of the light as the day gets darker. This gets even more pronounced in old age. At dusk, everything begins to get gray, and it's very hard to see vehicles with certain colors, as they blend into the background. You would be amazed at how important the color of your car is when poor visibility hits. This is one of the major causes of road accidents.

During dusk, it becomes very difficult to see silver or gray cars because everything looks gray. Similarly, it's difficult to see a white car when there's snow in the background. It's also difficult to see a green car when the scenery is full of green trees. Here's a very simple solution: adapt to the changing light conditions early by putting on your headlights at least thirty minutes before dusk. Many people already know this, but no one really cares. A few states have laws about having your lights on when you have your wipers on, or having your lights on if you are in a construction zone. But there are not many laws concerning the use of lights at dusk.

When it's raining hard and visibility is tough, I flash my lights at other vehicles, trying to communicate to them to turn on their lights. I am only trying to help them, so they can be seen. Some people get the hint, but others don't. It's quite simple: turn on your lights, so other drivers can see you. Develop the habit of being the first to turn on your lights as the day begins to darken.

Another problem is the design of modern cars. They now make daytime running lights, so they may be on, your dash lights are on, and you therefore think your lights are on—but they are not, and you still do not have tail lights on. So, whenever you're driving during dusk, you have to be absolutely sure that your lights are actually on. It's dangerous when other drivers can't see you, because they may change lanes and pull in front of you recklessly. This could lead to an accident, which is yet another reason why your eyes should always be sharp and moving when you're driving. Always look out for danger, so you can react as swiftly as the situation demands.

When talking about visibility, one thing always amazes me: some people wear dark clothing when taking a walk, or walking their dog. Please consider buying a high-visibility vest and wearing it when walking at night. It might save your life and help drivers see you earlier.

While we're talking about time, did you know that as you get older, your eyes change? When was the last time you had an eye exam? Because of my CDL license and being that I take blood pressure meds, I have to have a physical test every year to keep my CDL current. That physical includes an eye exam. Because I get new glasses every year, my eyes are so sharp that I can see for miles. (Check out the song "I Can See for Miles" by the rock band The Who.)

I'm so grateful for my eyes. They're so sharp that sometimes I feel like I can see into the future. You probably would feel the same way, too, if you took good care of your eyes, and did your physicals regularly. I have imagined actually being able to see into the future, but I'm convinced it would make life really boring. I mean, that's the beauty and excitement of life, right? We all need that uncertainty of the future to maintain a positive, expectant attitude.

So, the lesson from this exit is to remember to slow down a little when driving at dusk. Give your eyes a little extra time to adjust, turn on your lights, and try listening to Alabama's song, "Give Me One More Shot."

Memories of Exit 18

- Be an early adopter and turn your headlights on as dusk settles in.
- Get an eye exam every once in a while.
- Wear a high-visibility vest when walking at night.

EXIT 18A

ROASTING OR GRILLING VEGETABLES WELL DONE

For centuries, people have been roasting and grilling vegetables. Potatoes are the most common, but you can roast almost any other veggie. There is a bar here in Saratoga, called Brook Tavern, that serves roasted brussels sprouts as one of their happy hour specials. They serve it with balsamic vinegar, brown sugar, and bacon fat. This meal is out of this world, and each time I go there, I don't ever miss out on it. I've replicated the meal at home a few times, and although it's not quite as good as theirs, it's not bad for a novice. So, as far as roasting goes, let's start with brussels sprouts.

Next time you make bacon, save the bacon fat. Preheat the oven to 400 degrees. Buy a bag of fresh or frozen brussels sprouts and cut them in half. Put them in a bowl with a decent amount of olive oil, melted bacon fat, garlic powder, salt, pepper, and a splash of real maple syrup. Slosh them all around so they are well covered, then put them on a baking sheet. Salt and pepper them generously and roast them until they are almost starting to burn. This should take roughly forty-five minutes, but keep an eye on them. At this point, around two thirds of the outer leaves should be starting to get almost burnt. Take them out of the oven, toss them in a bowl with some crumbled bacon and some bacon fat, then throw a drizzle of balsamic vinegar on them. They are out of this world.

A couple years ago, we bought a grilling pan—essentially, a frying pan with holes in it and a removable handle. It's great for roasting any kind of vegetable on the grill. We roast sliced zucchini, pepper slices, thick-sliced onions, sliced beets, and any other kind of veggie. If you really love life, you should eat more veggies. Any recipe that helps you eat more veggies is a recipe that helps you live longer. Don't sleep on it.

One of the things that I have wanted to make for quite some time, but haven't gotten around to doing, is roasting potatoes on an open fire. When I was ten or twelve years old, I used to do it all the time. It's so simple: buy a bag of potatoes, wrap up four or five individually in an aluminum foil, build a nice campfire, then throw the potatoes in the red coals at the bottom of the fire for a half hour. After that, bring them out, let them cool a bit, peel the outer coat, cut the roasted potatoes into your desired size, and enjoy.

How about roasted garlic? Grab a head of garlic, slice off the top, pour some olive oil on it, and roast for 45 minutes at 350 degrees. Toward the end, throw some good, crunchy, Italian bread in the oven. When done and the garlic cools off, squeeze each clove of the roasted garlic onto slices of the bread, add a little salt and pepper, and enjoy!

When thinking about making soup, a wonderful way to start is by "roasting" whatever vegetables you are using in the oven or on the grill. A couple weeks ago I made a delicious carrot soup, starting with roasting carrots, onions, and celery in the oven.

The other day, our daughter Shannon surprised us with a different kind of sweet potato dish. She started by slicing a few large sweet potatoes around a quarter inch thick. She slathered them in olive oil, salt, and pepper, then put them on the gas grill, letting each side roast on low for about eight to ten minutes. Next, she put them in a baking dish and added butter and a garnish of sliced scallions. It was a very tasty, creative, and healthy dish, with some nice-looking grill marks. Roasting veggies is so fun. You can also use this pattern to make kale chips, but while you're at it, remember to throw in a few chopped-up walnuts on those sweet potatoes.

Here's a fun song by the band Alabama, "Song of the South."

Memories of Exit 18A

- Roast some veggies in the oven or on the grill with butter, salt, and pepper.
- Next time you are ever at a campfire, wrap some potatoes in aluminum foil and throw them in the red-hot coals for a half or three quarters of an hour. Be careful getting them out; they will be really hot.

EXIT 19

A QUITTER NEVER WINS AND A WINNER NEVER QUITS.

Your thoughts are powerful. There are many books out there that teach about the power of thoughts, and how to control them. If you want something to happen, think about it first, then start working on it. Then, it might just happen. Everything starts with a thought, dream, idea or whatever label you want to put on it. Years ago, I read about the four things you needed to have to be successful at something. It's from the book *Think and Grow Rich* by Napoleon Hill. They are:

- Burning desire. Weak desire brings weak results, just as a small fire makes a small amount of heat.
- Create an organized plan, and be willing to refine that plan. A dream without a plan is just a wish; you must take action.
- Be prepared for adversity. It's an inevitable part of life, so find the good in every situation.

- Create a team. You are going to need help, so get some good people around you.

I think the most important thing is the "taking action" part. You can have all the dreams you want, but you have to take action before you can actualize them. You must be motivated to work on whatever it is that you are trying to accomplish.

Believe me, I know sometimes it's more fun to laze and play around than to actually get to work on reaching your goals. But like I said before, interests are what keeps you happy. If you are working on an idea that will potentially change your life for the better, believe me: you will enjoy the ride and find happiness in the process.

Carpenters cut wood, electricians pull wire, sheet rockers sheetrock, roofers roof, teachers teach, managers manage, chefs cook, landscapers mow, designers design, doctors diagnose, actors act, musicians play, and bartenders serve drinks—and many of them find a way to have fun while they're at it. Whatever it is you're working on, you have to find a way to find happiness in it. Interests are what keeps humans happy. Take small, daily steps toward your goal. Get brave, take that step, and keep on growing. Work on your goal every day, even if it's a little. You will be creating a new habit, and in the long run, those small habits will launch you into a wonderful new life.

Create a good habit today. Smile, be more thankful, think more positively about the future, wag more, and bark less. You can change your life into a very exciting and fulfilling one. All you have to do is decide now. It may seem impossible, but you never know what's around the next corner. Miracles happen on a daily basis. Life is always changing. Just like the position of the sun and the moon change; just like the weather and seasons. Circumstances change, things change, people change, your life can also change. But you need to put in the work first.

Every day, when you wake up, make some affirmative declarations. Speak to yourself, saying, "Something great is going to happen in my life today." John Maxwell, the famous motivational speaker, once said that we should never let what we cannot do keep us from doing what we can do.

I think it's time to listen to "All I Need is a Miracle" by Mike and The Mechanics.

Memories of Exit 19

- Take some action toward achieving your dream every day.
- Consider reading *Think and Grow Rich* by Napoleon Hill. It's an oldie, but a goodie.
- Remember, be like Winston Churchill and "never give up."

EXIT 19A

STUFFED HAMBURGERS! (HAPPINESS 101)

I know red meat is bad for you. My son-in-law, who is in the medical field, always says, "If there was a perfect diet, everyone would be on it. There are vegetarians, and there are carnivores, and there are many people who eat everything. But what matters most is making healthy eating choices most of the time."

Meanwhile, if you are going to eat hamburgers, this is the only way: garlic stuffed hamburgers. Apart from garlic-stuffed hamburgers, there are also onion-stuffed hamburgers, sautéed spinach–stuffed hamburger, broccoli-stuffed, cheese-stuffed, caramelized onion–stuffed, olive-stuffed, ham-stuffed, shallot-stuffed, blue cheese–stuffed, butter-stuffed, and lobster-stuffed hamburgers. There are so many ways to stuff and enjoy the common, wonderful hamburger.

We happen to like garlic-stuffed more than the others. Start by making thinner-than-usual hamburger patties. Chop a few cloves of garlic and put them on top of the first patty, then put the other patty on top and squeeze the edges around the perimeter. Throw them on the grill and enjoy. Once you get the hang of the garlic version, you can get creative and try others. Here's a side note: when you start using cheese as a stuffing, you have to ensure that the burgers are properly done. It's similar to making Chicken Cordon Bleu, but, this time, with a burger. Get creative and try something new—maybe stuffing a burger with lobster.

While we're talking about stuffing, stuffed flounder is one of the most wonderful dishes. You should try it. Here's one of the fun versions you can make easily. Finely chop a shallot, open a can of chopped clams, and add a few pats of melted butter on it. Add a generous splash of dry white wine and mix them with bread crumbs until you get the desired consistency. Oil a baking pan, put down a piece of flounder, add a batch of the above stuffing, and place another piece of flounder on top. Add a little squeeze of fresh lemon and a dusting of paprika, then throw it in the oven. This chopped-clams stuffing also works for making stuffed mushrooms.

How about jalapeños stuffed with goat cheese, bacon, and shrimp? Deborah makes stuffed red peppers quite often, especially when the garden is in full bloom. It's so easy. She starts by cutting the top of the pepper off, cleaning out the seeds, and parboiling them for ten minutes. Then she browns up a pound of meatball mix, adds chopped onion, chopped garlic, grating cheese, and a little tomato sauce. She cooks the mixture for ten minutes, then stuffs the peppers with the mixture. She adds a tablespoon of sauce and a teaspoon of grating cheese to the top of each one, then bakes them at 350 degrees for thirty minutes. You know what happens next? She warms up some crusty Italian bread in the oven, gets out the garlic butter, and pours out two glasses of pinot noir for us to enjoy.

When you are flipping those burgers, listen to The Byrds song "Turn! Turn! Turn!"

Memories of Exit 19A

- Make some stuffed hamburgers, stuffed peppers, and stuffed flounder.
- Just stuff something!

EXIT 20

TRAVELING MAN

The most important thing about driving is being able to see. When you are driving, you are covering a lot of ground pretty fast. Always attempt to get the big picture, looking as far ahead as possible. If you are following a vehicle the same size as yours, you can see the brake lights of the car in front of them through their window glass. When following large vehicles, you can't see around them, so I always advise that you stay back an extra couple of car-lengths, so you won't ram into them if they slam their brakes suddenly. When following a small car, you can see the things they see, but that's not the case with bigger cars. So, if they have to brake suddenly, you may not have enough time to react appropriately.

It's especially very dangerous when it comes to road debris. If you are following too closely when the car in front of you goes over to the right suddenly, to dodge some debris in the middle of the road, you will not have time to react, and it could cause you some heavy damage. So, always keep your eyes moving, looking as far ahead as possible, so you'll get the big picture and can make decisions swiftly.

Learn how to use your mirrors more, as it helps you see who's around you and your best way out in an emergency. In situations like the one described above, if you know who is around you, you can go to the left or right, rather than slamming on the brakes.

Another nice trick is to drive a couple extra inches to the left in rush hour, bumper-to-bumper traffic, so you can see the brake lights of the cars further ahead. It's quite hard to do this when the sun is blazing and peering into your eyes, so keep a decent pair of shades in your vehicle to use when necessary. I always wonder why some drivers don't keep a decent pair of shades in their car. I feel like this should be so common, considering that the sun can actually blind you for a couple seconds.

Here's a few more things to note about driving in the sun: always consider the direction you're driving. Remember, if you live twenty or thirty miles west of where you work, you will possibly be driving into the sun every morning and driving back into the sun every evening, on your way home. It might not sound important to you right now, but driving into the sun on a daily basis is not fun at all. So, get your dark shades handy.

Enough about the sun. How about winter? If you live in an area where it snows quite often, I'll advise you to buy a house with the driveway facing south. That way, the sun will always help melt the driveway. Just open your driveway a little and let the sun do its work for a while. Sadly, you cannot say the same thing about having a driveway facing north, as that would get minimal sun. Having a south-facing driveway will also ensure that you don't have to scrape your windshield as much. Sometimes, you just have to scrape off the snow and face the car south while you let it warm up. When letting your car warm up and trying to defrost the windshield, put your sun visor down and crack the driver's window a quarter inch. The sun visor holds heat closer to the windshield, and cracking the window will release pressure.

Please start the habit of cleaning all the snow off your car in the winter. I mean, you have to be able to see where you are going. Get one of these newer, extendable snow brushes and always use it. I have seen a wreck caused by snow accumulation on a car. The driver did not clean the foot of snow off their roof, so five miles later, as the car warmed up, when they slammed the brakes, the snow slid forward and covered their windshield. They rammed into the car in front of them. That was a big price to pay for being lazy.

As I stated in one of the earlier exits, you are going to get distracted when driving. Try to get yourself in a situation where it is a little less dangerous before you entertain any distraction. In the same manner, try to keep yourself safe by being conscious of both the sun and the snow, so they don't cause you huge damages.

Now how about you check out the songs "Blinded by the Light" by Manfred Mann's Earth Band and "Cheap Sunglasses" by ZZ Top.

Memories of Exit 20

- Keep a pair of sunglasses in your car for whenever the sun gets in your eyes.
- Don't drive behind bigger vehicles that block your "big picture."

- Clean the snow off your car, and if you have the choice, park your car so the windshield faces south in the winter. You will be able to defrost the windshield quicker with the help of a little sunshine.

EXIT 20A

EGGPLANT PARM AND ITALIAN STRING BEANS

I sure do love eggplant Parmesan. This is Deb's mother's version, which our daughter, Shannon, now makes quite often. First, start by peeling and slicing a couple fresh eggplants, maybe between an eighth- or a quarter-inch thick. Soak them for a half an hour in a mixture of warm water and balsamic vinegar. After patting them dry, fry them lightly in vegetable oil for about three minutes on each side. When you are done, pat them dry again, and set aside.

In a separate pan, sauté two or three (more like five or six) chopped cloves of garlic in a little olive oil (don't burn them). Open and add a can of crushed Italian tomatoes, throw in half a cup of dry red wine, and cook on low heat for around fifteen minutes. We found a brand of Italian tomatoes called Mutti. You may want to try it out, as the taste is wholesome and ancient.

Grab a baking pan and coat the bottom with the above sauce. Add a layer of the fried eggplant, sprinkle a dusting of Italian breadcrumbs, and add an eighth of an inch of fresh grated Parmesan or Romano. Repeat the four items three times. After the third layer of fresh grating cheese, add one more layer of sauce and cover the top with sliced cheddar or fresh mozzarella, and generous amounts of chopped, fresh parsley. Bake at 350 degrees for an hour. Toward the end, put a chunk of Italian bread in the oven.In a small bowl, add some olive oil, crushed red pepper, and Italian seasoning for dipping your bread. Put out an assortment of olives, open a cab or a merlot, and enjoy.

Another nice version of eggplant is to slice it thin, dip it in flour, egg wash, and breadcrumbs and fry until golden brown. You can also just put it in the oven. After it cools, mix up a couple of different dipping sauces like soy sauce, guacamole, hummus, honey mustard, or a garlic, caper, shallot, and mayo mixture.

I love making Italian string beans like this: Start by cooking frozen, French-cut string beans following the directions on the package. You then strain them, put them in a baking pan and make a mixture of bread crumbs, garlic, grating cheese, olive oil, and a little butter. Add the mixture to the string beans, mix well, dust the top with a little more grating cheese, and bake for fifteen minutes. Just like eggplant, string bean recipes are unbelievably better the next day. You can also use this recipe to make broccoli, peas, squash, zucchini or any other veggie of your choice.

Talking about Italian stuff, why not listen to a great Italian singer! YouTube Andrea Bocelli and Celine Dion singing "The Prayer."

Memories of Exit 20 A

- Use more olive oil, butter, garlic, breadcrumbs, lemon, and good Italian grating cheese when preparing your veggies. These items add great texture and flavor.

EXIT 21

REST AREA NEXT RIGHT

Let's talk about rest. Do you realize that your mind and brain are always working, 'round the clock? How about you stop for a moment to get some rest and get rid of some of the waste in your mind? Life is tough and stressful. If you want to live a happy and healthy life, it's important to prioritize your rest and dispose of your mind's waste regularly. Just as the body gets rid of physical waste frequently, the mind also needs to ease itself of its waste regularly. Imagine what would happen to your body if you don't defecate or urinate for many days. That's exactly how uncomfortable, sick, and toxic your mind will be if you allow its wastes to keep accumulating.

First thing, get rid of all anger. For your sake, you need to learn to let go. When people do things that get you angry, try to get over it as quickly as possible. It's a very healthy trait to forgive and forget, not just for the sake of the offender, but for your inner peace. Deborah and I would not still be together after fifty years if we both didn't have the traits of forgiving and forgetting quickly. Life is not stagnant. When you breathe in, you exhale. When you eat and drink, you know what happens. So, when someone offends you, you have to also, naturally, let it slide off your mind.

Thoughts will always pop into your mind. Some of them, you'll like; some of them, you won't. Get rid of the ones you don't like as quickly as possible. I mean, you take out the garbage in your house every other day. Why would you want to let the garbage in your heart remain there for so long? If you want to protect your happiness, you need to have "selective memory." Forget the negative that makes you sad, and remember only the positive that fills you with joy. It's not that hard to do. It's just a decision.

Some people find it extremely hard to forget things that hurt them. They hold on to their past so much that it prevents them from moving forward, and from basking in the present and future. You have to mentally train yourself to realize that the hurt you're holding on to is not worth wasting your time on earth thinking about it. The world is moving at an incredibly fast pace. Why do you want to remain chain-bound to a rock from your past?

Many people are way too judgmental. They always have some fault to point out, no matter how hard people try. Maybe in their head, they regard themselves as some kind of king or queen who has been bestowed with the supreme power to pass judgment on everyone. For some reason, they think they can control other people's lives, and they are constantly wrecking family relationships. If you're that kind of person, you should be tired of that toxic lifestyle by now. Are you not tired? Is your life so perfect that you feel like you have the right to meddle into everyone else's affairs? Well, I have news for you. As long as you continue wasting your time on judging other people, your own life won't get better, because you're not channeling your time into judicious use. Learn to live and let live. Don't try to control other people's lives.

I understand that you may have formed this habit over time, and it may be difficult for you to stop, but you have to work on it constantly and deliberately, every day. Let other people have their own lives so you can fix yours. One of my favorite sayings is, "I would rather be happy than right." I am beyond being judgmental. I'm a "live and let live" kind of guy, so when someone wants me to get involved in some kind of judgmental conversation, I always ask them, "What day is it?" Let's imagine they say, "Sunday." I'd answer, "I don't make any judgmental statements on Sundays."

I am repeating myself once again for a reason: stop being so judgmental. Stop constantly judging other people's actions, dreams, speech, life, whatever. In fact, stop constantly judging yourself, too! Try to be a little more like a Buddhist monk. Live, breathe, and think peace. Listen to John Lennon's song, "Give Peace a Chance."

Earlier, we discussed the importance of smiling. It's a shame, but some people have a hard time with it. I know you have a lot going on, but life is already so hard. You have to be able to laugh at yourself sometimes. You simply just have to decide, some days, to have fun, goof around, and not worry about anything. Everyone faces ups and downs because that is the nature of life. Life can't always be great. Sometimes, it will bring you so much sadness—other times, it brings you joy. One thing is for sure: life is temporary, and so are its challenges. You came into this world and you will someday go out of this world. If you are religious, you have peace because you believe in the afterlife. If you're not religious, find a way to make peace with it because as the saying goes, "There are no atheists in a foxhole."

Life can bring you many problems on a day-to-day basis. In order to be mentally healthy, there are days when you have to block the problems out and say, "Today, I won't worry about anything. I won't entertain any negative energy." Be deliberate about it, and map out these days as your happy days. Stress is very bad for you. The day-to-day pressure of life increases everyone's stress level, so you have to remember to take care of yourself. Make conscious efforts to prioritize self-care. Go out to have fun often, and stay away from people who are always bearers of bad news.

If these people try to contact you on your happy day, tell them you are having a personal emergency, and that you'll get back to them later. Spend the day doing whatever makes you happy. Let your fairytale imagination run wild that day, and *trick* yourself into being happy. Believe it or not, some people are suffering from so much self-inflicted pressure that they can't let go of their pain and bitterness. Don't be like them. Be thankful, relax, and have fun. You can always go back to worrying later (but I suggest you don't).

Life is full of mysteries. To navigate them and maintain happiness, you have to have faith and the ability to believe that good things will happen, even when there are no physical or mental facts to support it. Have faith in me when I tell you to take a whole day to be thankful, have fun, and not worry about anything. Just like your body needs a rest, so does your brain. Rejuvenate your brain quite often. Enjoy the moment and don't worry about anything. Eat, drink, and be merry—or do whatever it is that you do to "chill."

While at it, turn up Bobby McFerrin's timeless song, "Don't Worry, Be Happy."

Memories of Exit 21

- Take out the garbage in your brain. If you throw away a piece of pizza in the garbage, you wouldn't get it out to eat a couple of days later—yet, many people keep bringing up old garbage in their brain.
- Remember, your mind needs a rest now and then. It's refreshing to take a break from all the stress.
- Start having a selective memory. Remember the good stuff, and once you throw away the bad stuff, don't bring it back.

EXIT 21A

STEAK AU POIVRE

I am not a big steak guy. Don't get me wrong, I have been known to grill up a New York strip or a filet on the BBQ now and then, but there are quite a few dinners that I would rather enjoy—like meatballs and spaghetti, chicken parm, a nice soup, a huge spinach salad with some toasted garlic bread on the side, or any type of fish. Half the time, I would rather have a good burger than a steak.

I think there are too many variables when buying a steak. I hate spending big money on a steak and then it turns out to be very tough. I guess that is why I spend just a little more and get the New York strip or filet. Or, you can buy the "porterhouse" and get both.A great way to save money when you are buying a filet mignon for steak is to buy the whole tenderloin at BJ's or Costco and have the butcher clean it up. You can choose the thickness of your steaks and freeze them individually in any quantity you like. You can then use the smaller parts for stir fry or soup. Remember to ask the butcher to give you all the fat he took off. You can use the fat for the base of a sauce.

Last summer, we were up in Bar Harbor, Maine, at our son-in-law's family cabin, planning dinner for twelve people. We went to a local supermarket called Hannaford to get some steak. At the butcher counter, I noticed the filets were $24.95 per pound. I was able to strike a deal with the butcher, and he gave us a whole tenderloin at $17.99 per pound. We got more than fifteen beautiful steaks for around $150. Moral to the story is, always ask the butcher for a deal and buy a whole tenderloin.

When it comes to preparing steak, there is one thing I always do: I make a beautiful "steak au poivre" sauce. This recipe is a wonderful way to pan fry steak with a peppercorn sauce. The first time you make this, it is best to just make a little portion that would serve as dinner for two. Repeat it a few times; after you've gotten a hang of it, you can then make it for a larger number of people.

Open a container of beef stock, pour a cup in a small pot, and keep it on low heat on the back of the stove. You will need an adjustable pepper grinder, because you have to start the dish by coating two New York strips or filets with a good covering of coarsely ground fresh pepper on both sides. Make sure to pat it in properly. Then, put a small amount of oil in a regular pan and fry the steaks on higher heat for a couple minutes on each side.

You are not fully cooking them at this time. You are just browning them a little to get some fat and flavor for the sauce. You could also use some of the fat the butcher gave to you. After browning each side for a couple minutes, remove them from the pan and put them on a plate.

Add about a half cup of the beef broth, scraping up the fond (the small brown particles that stuck to the pan). Add a few finely chopped shallots, one finely chopped clove of garlic, and a half teaspoon of Dijon mustard to the pan and simmer for ten minutes. Now it's time to start drizzling in a quarter cup of brandy and cooking the alcohol off little by little. When you're done, add half a cup of heavy cream and put the steaks back in the pan on low heat.

Continue spooning the sauce over the steaks for five minutes, then check the steaks to know if they're done. When the steaks are a little rarer than you like, remove them from the pan and cover them in tin foil while you finish the sauce. You have to decide how thick your sauce will be. If you want it thinner, add more beef stock and another splash of heavy cream. If you want it thicker, turn up the heat and allow it to reduce and thicken. When you like the consistency, plate up your steak and a beautiful baked potato and cover them in the sauce. You can also pair this meal with steamed asparagus.

This recipe rocks! Why not YouTube Bob Seger's "Like a Rock."

Memories of Exit 21A

- When you want to make steaks, ask for a deal, and buy the whole tenderloin.
- Try this "steak au poivre" sauce. It's a really fun meal.
- When you want to learn more about making sauces, use YouTube.
- You get better at something by doing it over and over.

EXIT 22

PARK PLACE

Whenever you are picking someone up or dropping someone off when driving, always put the vehicle in "park" (or, if driving standard, "neutral" with the emergency brake on). The reason for this is that if the car is in drive or reverse and your foot slips off the brake while that person is halfway out the door, they could get seriously injured.

Many crazy things can happen all at once when you are driving. When that person is getting in or out of the car, someone walking by could interrupt you by asking directions. A car can pull up next to you and ask you to move. The phone could ring. A passenger in the backseat could start trying to tell you what to do, or your wife or husband could start telling you that what you are doing is wrong. You could very easily take your foot off the brake, and many things could go wrong.

It's very important to remember this rule, to save someone from a big injury. It becomes even more critical in cold or wet weather. If the vehicle is cold, it could still be running on high idle so it would require more foot pressure on the brake to stop it. If your shoe or the brake pedal is wet or slippery, your leg could slip off. Imprint this at the back of your mind for optimal safety of your passengers. Always put the vehicle in park (or neutral, with emergency brake on) when someone is entering or exiting your vehicle.

While we're talking about habits, when you are parked at a strip mall where you have to back out to leave, please do it very slowly. Look for pedestrians, motorcycles, bicycles, and cars. Cars are big, and aren't hard to see while turning your head and constantly checking your mirrors, but you still need to pay attention so you can see motorcycles, bicycles, and pedestrians. There are many blind spots, so go slow. It's a good thing that cars now come with reverse cameras, but you need to also look over your shoulder and use your mirrors to be absolutely sure that there's nothing in your path.

I believe it's way safer to park in a spot that you don't have to reverse out of when leaving. If you are ever visiting someone's house, especially if you are arriving in daylight and leaving after dark, it's best to back in while it's daylight so you can just drive away later, after dark. This parking style is called combat parking. You can also choose a spot where you don't have to do any backing up at all. If you go to a party or big gathering and you have to back out at night, you should first walk around to make sure there is nothing behind you.

As the old Boy Scout motto says, "Be prepared." In an automobile, it's very important to be prepared. You should always have an emergency kit, as you never can tell when you'll need it. All you really need is an old milk crate or cooler filled with a bunch of necessities in your trunk. Here's a list of things you need:

1. A gallon of drinkable water
2. A roll of paper towels and some Windex
3. Flashlight with an extra set of batteries
4. Extra car phone charger
5. Blanket
6. Flares or triangles
7. Sunglasses
8. Can of nuts
9. Jug of good windshield washer fluid (the expensive de-ice kind if you live up north)
10. Quart of oil and a jug of antifreeze
11. Business card of your mechanic or tow company
12. Old jacket
13. Smaller cheap tarp (two or three bucks at Home Depot)
14. Tool kit (channel locks, multi-bit screwdriver, hammer, and bigger pry bar)
15. Snow shovel, if you live up north
16. Your AAA membership
17. Well-inflated spare tire
18. A little battery-powered air pump to pump up a low tire
19. A high-visibility vest in case you break down at night

To increase visibility, another great idea is to only hang clothes on the driver's side behind the driver. When you hang clothes in the backseat on the passenger side, you decrease your ability to see cars in that area when you quickly look over your shoulder.

Make a change, listen to Michael Jackson's "Man in the Mirror."

Memories of Exit 22

- Put the car in park when picking up or dropping someone off.
- Take your time when backing out of any parking spot, even at the mall.
- Combat park whenever you can.
- Hang clothes behind the driver, and adjust your side mirrors out a little further.

EXIT 22A

THE POISON SYRUP AND THE GMO CARB

There sure is a huge market for soda. Many overweight people drink it every day. It never ceases to amaze me how many drinks with tons of high fructose corn syrup people consume. When I was driving a tractor trailer for a living, every day someone from our company brought 280,000 pounds (four loads) of high fructose corn syrup from the rail yard in Albany to the Pepsi plant in Latham. That's over a quarter million pounds of high fructose corn syrup every day! On holidays, I would see many of the employees at Pepsi coming around to the back to get their free, two cases of soda to take home—regular or diet, which is worse? Sad to say, many of them were overweight

We also delivered thousands of pounds of high fructose corn syrup to Bimbo in Albany. Bimbo is one of the largest bread manufacturers in America. They make many different brands of generic bread. If you would read labels, you'd realize that there is high fructose corn syrup in almost every processed food we eat.

Yes, I confess, I have been to McDonald's, and have heard the person in front of me ask for two Big Macs, a large fry, and a *Diet* Coke. Walk down the aisle in your local food store and just about every drink has either sugar in it, or it's "diet," which is even worse. The chemicals they use to make a soda "diet" are foreign to our body, so our bodies reject it and store it as fat. You cannot lose weight drinking any diet product because the chemicals it's made from somehow make you hungrier.

Once again, I am not a saint. I drink alcohol, which isn't the healthiest drink out there, but I never drink soda or fruit juices with high fructose corn syrup. Here is the best drink you could possibly drink: WATER! Yes, it gets boring, but there are a few healthy things you could add to it to make it more fun. The first thing that comes to mind is lemon, or how about some lime? You can also infuse a few slices of fresh cucumber. You can make homemade green tea, and maybe add a little splash of vodka if that's your thing.

One of my favorite drinks is still Miller Light, a can of confidence. If you ever see Bolthouse Farms brand carrot juice, try it. It's expensive but really delicious. While taking a sip of any of these drinks, go on YouTube and find the song "Why We Drink" by Justin Moore.

If you are constantly having problems with gaining weight, a great way to become healthier is to stop using sugar in your coffee and breakfast cereal. Also, stop drinking any liquid that contains high fructose corn syrup. Eat more high fiber foods, stop eating French fries and white bread. These changes alone can save you a thousand calories a day.

You should also take a walk every day. While you are taking that walk, listen to the Grateful Dead's song "Goin' Down the Road Feeling Bad."

Memories of Exit 22A

- Before you buy any food at the supermarket, read the ingredients to see if it has any high fructose corn syrup in it.

EXIT 23

ALL I NEED IS A MIRACLE

Our lives are amazing. Think about all the wonderful achievements humans have made in the last 100 years. Just think about the milestones in medicine alone! I had my hip replaced eight years ago, and it still feels brand new. I had my carotid arteries in my neck cleaned out twice, to reduce the risk of having a stroke because of plaque buildup. I have a stent in my iliac artery to increase blood flow to my left leg. I am presently recuperating from a total knee replacement I had in March of 2024. Bionic man over here, thanks to advancements in medicine. Fifty years ago, I would have been dead from a stroke already.

From the Industrial Revolution of machines, trains, automobiles, electricity, and refrigeration to the technology of today, it's unbelievable. I mean, Chuck Yeager broke the sound barrier almost seventy-five years ago. Man first landed on the moon over fifty years ago. Now we have artificial intelligence, where computers are smarter than humans. When I just had my knee replaced, part of the surgery was robotic! Many aspects of our lives are changing at an exponential rate. We are living in a miraculous time in history.

Who knows what advancements are in store for our future? While the future is unknown, we should not fear it. Instead, always think of the most positive possibility, because miracles happen constantly in life. I mean, life is a miracle in itself. There are many concepts that the human mind cannot conceive. For instance, when you point your finger toward the sky and say, "That's the sky," how far can you go before you touch it? How many millions or trillions of miles can you go before you reach *there?* Where does space end? Does it end? Think about the word "eternity." Why is it that time is never ending? Think about the temperature of the earth for a moment—I mean, humans can only live from around zero to a hundred degrees Fahrenheit. What if the earth was a hundred degrees warmer or colder? Would there still be life?

One of the most beautiful and exciting things about life is that you never know what's in store for you, or what's around the corner waiting for you. When I wake up every morning, I say, "Something wonderful is going to happen today." (It already did, because I woke up next to the person I love the most, my wife, Deborah). Life is a gamble, and we are all still in the game. Every day you wake up, you just have to keep playing the game, and be happy that you're here. When I was driving a tractor trailer, I did not like getting up at five in the morning, driving forty-five minutes to work, and then working for twelve to fourteen hours a day (common hours in the trucking industry). But I was thankful that I could still do it, and it was pretty heavy entertainment. Now, I can no longer do that, but I'm grateful for the things I can do now. That's the beauty of life; you never know what's around the next corner.

I think a big part of mental health and happiness is believing that it's a good world. I have happiness from within, but I constantly run into many amazing people that help me believe the world is beautiful. You have to have faith, which sometimes means believing in something you cannot understand. You have to have hope. Believe in miracles, my friend—they happen every day.

Like the old Alabama song says, "Give Me One More Shot," I'll give it all I got. While streaming that song, check out "Humble and Kind" by Tim McGraw.

Memories of Exit 23

- Believe that it's a good world.
- Believe in miracles, because they happen every day. It's a miracle that it is 2024 and we are all still alive.

EXIT 23A

ADD SOME WONDERFUL INGREDIENTS

There are quite a few common food items that you can add to any recipe to make them tastier and more exciting. By now, you already know about my excessive compulsion for chopping things. Whenever I am making any dish, I am always chopping something, be it shallots, garlic, peppers, celery, carrots, etc. Here are a couple of things you should get in the habit of using more: parsley (easy to grow on a windowsill), Italian tomato paste from a tube, anchovy paste from a tube, soy sauce, chopped scallions, mustard (always add a little to scrambled eggs), finely chopped nuts, good grating cheese, fresh grated lemon zest, fresh grated ginger, and breadcrumbs. Don't forget that splash of A1 when you are making a Bloody Mary!

What is in your spice rack? Try some new spices that are not in your normal everyday use. There are quite a few different types of salt you can try, even more than I mention here. Regular table salt is the most refined salt and is typically bleached to make it white. Many of the other salts like Kosher (larger crystals and crunchy), sea salt, fleur de sel, grey salt, (all from seawater), and Himalayan pink, are not refined and have more trace minerals.

There are quite a few different types of pepper, also. I love coarsely ground, multicolored peppercorns. Have you ever tried white pepper? It has a slightly different taste than black pepper. Try some red pepper flakes on something for a little excitement.

It is so much fun to experiment with some new tastes. Just to mention a few:

- Parsley
- Sage
- Rosemary
- Thyme
- Basil
- Bay leaves
- Paprika
- Oregano
- Cumin
- Turmeric
- Chili powder
- Cilantro
- Dill
- Ginger
- Cinnamon

Here is a great paprika trick, and a simple fast way to make great home fries. I learned this about fifty years ago, while I was at an auto race at Watkins Glen, NY. In a certain area, there were food concessions with lines as long as a hundred feet. They were selling a paper bowl full of home fries for a buck. I still use this recipe once in a while for breakfast.

Open a can of diced potatoes and drain them well. After draining, dump them on a paper plate and scoop the potatoes out of the plate to the frying pan to leave behind some of the sludge. Heat them up in tons of melted butter with a heavy hit of paprika to make them look browned. That's all—your delicious, five-minute home fries. They go incredibly well with over-easy eggs instead of toast.

Remember the mustard I mentioned up there? You can use it instead of an egg wash when you are frying thinly sliced chicken or pork chops. Dip the thinly sliced chicken or pork in flour, then coat one side with mustard (Maille), dip it in a mixture of breadcrumbs and very finely chopped cashews, coat the upside with mustard, flip over, coat the other side, then fry until lightly browned. It's a yummy delicacy. I have made this "steak au poivre" sauce many times. It's essentially a brown peppercorn sauce. You need beef stock (low salt, if you are going to reduce a lot), beef drippings, shallots, brandy, garlic, heavy cream, and a little mustard, reduced for quite a while.

Here are a few tips to make things a little simpler. A sauce is a mixture of a liquid (typically an oil) and a solid that is then reduced to thicken and become more flavorful. Oil and water typically do not mix, so when making a sauce, you sometimes need an emulsifier or bigger particles to keep the water and oil from separating. The most common emulsifiers are egg yolk and mustard. A great way to thicken a sauce is to make a Béchamel (a mixture of flour and a fat), and add it to the sauce as a thickener. A couple weeks ago, I made true Beurre Blanc, and it came out excellent. I want you to also start trying out these recipes. After trying them a few times, you, too, will become good at it.

Try something new! Listen to "City of New Orleans" written by Steve Goodman, performed by Willie Nelson (The Highwaymen also do a great version).

Memories of Exit 23A

Try some new spices.

EXIT 24

DON'T FORGET YOUR KEYS!

When I used to deliver diesel fuel to companies with a truck fleet, there were big signposts at the exit of their yard that said, "Don't forget your keys." These signs weren't referring to just your car keys. They refer to five keys, namely:

- Aim high in steering
- Get the big picture
- Keep your eyes moving
- Make sure they see you
- Have a way out

Personally, I'll add a couple more:

- Check your mirrors often.
- Don't let your passengers put their feet on the dashboard (if you get in an accident, the airbag will go off and break their legs and hips).

- When you arrive at an intersection or stop sign, look both ways to see if it's clear before you proceed. Look in the direction of worse visibility last.

Look at the shortest vision path last. If you look to the right and you can see around 1000 feet, then look to the left and you can only see fifty feet because of a curve or a crest in a hill, always remember to look at the shorter vision direction one last time before you move.

Try to anticipate what is going to happen within the next few seconds and minutes. Imagine that you are in the middle lane of a three-lane interstate, and a tractor trailer is up ahead of you on the right as you approach an entrance ramp. You look ahead and see another car approaching the entrance, to join the interstate. You should know that the tractor trailer is probably going to signal and attempt to switch to the middle lane, so he doesn't have to slow down for the car. Anticipate these moves and let them guide your decisions whenever you're driving.

Now let's talk about tickets. Are there ticket-evading tactics? First thing you should know is that state troopers, sheriffs, and police officers are just like me and you. They have a job, except they risk their lives on a typical day helping and protecting you. They have to go to family disputes where someone is drunk and waving a loaded gun around. They have to go to robbery scenes where someone is shooting at them. They are called to tragic traffic accidents where there are body parts lying around, and other people are trapped in their cars screaming for help because it's on fire. Sometimes I wonder how they can sleep at night after dealing with the stuff they do.

Police officers have more important things to do than traffic enforcement, but that's part of their job. Believe it or not, they are trying to keep the roads safe. Do you know you can make their job easier? Yeah, it's quite simple: don't do stupid stuff.

If you do a pre-trip once in a while, you'll notice when your headlight, taillight, brake light, or signal light goes bad. Possibly you'll notice when your registration or inspection sticker becomes overdue. Perhaps you'll notice that your emergency brake cable is dragging on the ground, or you have a low tire. But the biggest risk of getting a ticket comes with speeding. The only time it is safe to speed is on an interstate. When you are doing more than twenty miles per hour over the speed limit, you're breaking the rules—but there's a way around it. Keep your eyes moving, looking for the man. Radar only works in a straight line.

They love to find creative places to hide—sitting in a turn around, behind an abutment, behind a tree, just over a crest in a hill, or on an entrance ramp where they can get you from behind. If you are traveling on a straight stretch of road with guardrails, there is really nowhere for them to hide. I always check up near the turnarounds—I mean, it's common sense. Some people like to use cars that pass them as a "rabbit" for coverage, figuring that they are the ones breaking ground and will be the ones to get caught. That's pretty smart, but I would follow them from quite a ways back, being polite. When you are speeding on an interstate, especially at night, always remember your back door. Be watchful for when someone is coming up behind you, to know if they're gaining on you suspiciously. If you notice that they are, it's best to check up, and let them pass, so you can be sure it's not the man trying to get you from behind.

If you ever get stopped, there are quite a few tips that will help you. First thing, always pull over to the right, ideally in an area where there are no guardrails so you can get off the road a little further and put on your four-way flashers. When the officer approaches your vehicle, stay in your vehicle, roll your window down, and keep your hands in plain sight. This is the most important thing: keep your hands in plain sight. You already know they're stopping you, so you should already know exactly where your license and registration are, and you should have them on the dash with your hands on top of the steering wheel in plain sight.

Having your paperwork ready and your hands in plain sight will ease the officers of a lot of stress. Be very courteous and have good manners, like saying "sir." Do not move too fast. Instead, always tell the officer what you are going to do before you do it. Something like, "Sir, I am going to look in my glove compartment for my registration and insurance card." You are worried about getting a ticket; they are worried about you having a gun.

After you give them the appropriate paperwork, they will ask you "Do you know why I pulled you over?" Be honest, have manners, and do not be disrespectful or sarcastic. When the conversation starts, a good thing to say is, "Sir, I am sorry, I know I made a mistake, can you see it in your heart to give me a break?" It's a good time to beg for forgiveness. Sorry to say this, but speeding tickets are a big percentage of creating cash flow for the town. Same as court costs, fines, and surcharges. So, yes, beg the law officer to not give you a ticket.

Change your beliefs. Police officers are humans, and they also have feelings. Always be very polite and respectful. They have family, children, etc., and are just doing their job, which is mostly helping people. If you are nice to them, you will increase the chances of them being nice to you!

Listen to Eric Clapton's version of "Key to the Highway."

Memories of Exit 24

- When driving, try to envision what's going to happen in the next couple seconds or minutes.
- If you ever get stopped by the police, keep your hands in plain sight and tell the officer what you are going to do before you do it. Be very nice and treat them with the utmost respect. Beg for forgiveness.
- Don't forget your keys, which are
  1. Aim high in your steering (look further ahead)
  2. Get the big picture
  3. Keep your eyes moving,
  4. Make sure they see you
  5. Have a way out

EXIT 24A

NON DIET
WANT TO STOP GAINING WEIGHT? YOU HAVE TO CHANGE YOUR HABITS.

Today is Sunday, January 7th, 2024. I will be seventy-four years old this coming Thursday. I am six feet tall and currently weigh around 215 pounds. For most of my life, I weighed around 185 pounds. I made the decision to quit smoking cigarettes in 2014, as it was ruining my health, and since then I have gained thirty to forty pounds. A couple weeks ago, sometime around Christmas, I was almost up to 225 pounds. I am going to lose some weight!

I drink alcohol. I know it has few calories, but I'm working toward reducing it further. One of my big downfalls is eating bread. I love warm Italian bread. I love toasting any kind of bread. Another problem is portion control. It's so much fun to eat massive quantities of good food and have a couple of drinks to go with it. Deborah, on the other hand, loves pasta so much that I call her a pastatute. I take her out for a spaghetti dinner as a romantic gesture.

Many of us are addicted to laziness, convenience, carbs, and sugar. This is why all the fast food joints do so well. The human body is a machine. Just like your car stops when you run out of gas, the body becomes weak when it finishes consuming fuel from the food you consumed. When this happens, in most cases, junk food, soft drinks, and fast food outlets are the nearest and easiest source of fuel. When we eat food, we burn it up. If you eat more than you burn, your body stores it as fat and you gain weight. If you burn more than you eat, you burn your stored fat (Ketosis) and lose weight. The more you move, the more you burn.

Weight loss is a billion-dollar industry. There are so many diet concepts that I could not begin to name them. Keto, low-carb, Mediterranean, Atkins, etc. I am sure they all work on some level, but many times, you lose some weight and then gain it right back, because these diets are not sustainable. In order to lose weight and keep it off, you have to change your eating habits—but then, who wants to be constantly hungry, and not eat? The simple solution is to get rid of the bad and introduce the good. Stop eating all the processed stuff and eat more foods off the low-carb, low-sugar list. Being that they are low-carb, low-sugar, you can eat massive quantities of them and not gain weight or stay hungry.

They include: eggs, avocados, almonds, walnuts, pecans, grass-fed meats, chicken breast (not fried), small portions of cheese, olives, apples, celery with organic peanut butter, cucumbers with guacamole, chia seeds, broccoli, cauliflower, brussels sprouts, kale, carrots, leafy lettuce, beets, asparagus and Swiss chard, grapefruits, lemons, onions, peppers, spinach, oatmeal, strawberries, snap peas, watermelons, tomatoes, zucchini, cabbage, mushrooms, arugula, sauerkraut, seaweed, collard greens, blueberries, raspberries, blackberries, and soups with any of the above veggies. Eating any of the above foods and you will be eating like a king.

YouTube "Riding with the King" by Eric Clapton and B.B. King. (Watch the official video.)

Memories of Exit 24A

- Try to eat more foods on this list.
- Watch your carbs (try to stay below fifty grams of carbs a day).
- Add herbs and spices, and change your eating habits in small increments at a time.
- Keep it simple—replace a bagel and cream cheese with a couple scrambled eggs and no bread. Replace French fries with some greens or soup, and realize you have to stop eating sweets, soda, potato chips, cheese puffs, Doritos, etc.

EXIT 25

DID YOU EVER SEE A BRINKS TRUCK FOLLOWING A HEARSE?

Around ten years ago I saw my neighbor, Dean, in his front lawn pulling weeds. I always saw him there, as he loved working on his nice lawn. I didn't know him well, but we did chat occasionally. So on that day, I stopped, rolled down the window, and said, "Yo, Dean, how are you doing, man?" We talked for a couple minutes. He was saying that the kids were all grown, he only had seven mortgage payments left, and he was feeling really good about life. Maybe he and his wife would downsize, maybe move, maybe not, but basically the fun fact was that he was going to be working less and would finally start enjoying life. We talked a little more, and I said, "God bless you man, see you later."

I drove off thinking, "Wow, what a lucky guy! House paid off. Man, where did I go wrong?" At the time, I was sixty-three and still buried in debt, working like a dog. Six months later, it was winter and my wife and I woke up to flashing red lights three houses away in the middle of the night. The next evening, on the way home from work, I saw my neighbor Brian and asked what was going on last night. He said it was a bad scene. Dean had passed away last night from a heart attack. Here was a guy in his late fifties, who had life by the balls… and then he dropped dead. It was very sad to hear.

Back in early March of 2015, two of my older brothers passed away within a couple of weeks. It's sad, very sad, but you have to get back on the horse and keep on moving. The lesson here is: every day you are alive, you have to celebrate like a freaking rock star. Smile—people like to be around happy people; they don't like to be around people who constantly complain. No matter what happens, as long as you are taking nourishment and standing upright, you are doing good. Always remember to keep a positive outlook, no matter how bad the circumstances are. Do things that make you happy, and do them now. Don't shift them till later. Remember, there's no "someday" on a calendar. The longer you wait for the future, the shorter it will be. Don't run yourself out of time.

Have you found the essence of your journey here on earth? If you haven't, I need you to read the book *Blue Zones* by Dan Beuttner. It contains some gems that'll help you to live longer. Read the book *Think and Grow Rich* by Napoleon Hill. You might have a world-changing idea.

Here are some things you should always do:

- Love somebody.
- Move your body more. Stretch, bend over, flex your muscles, get down on the floor and get back up ten times a day.
- Download the "Fitbit" app and walk ten thousand steps a day.

- Drink more water.
- You maintain your house, yard, car, clothes, and hopefully your body, but what about maintaining your brain, spirit, and relationships?
- Always wear your seatbelt, and don't let your passenger place their feet on the dashboard.

Here are a few questions you need to mull over: When was the last time you...

- Helped anyone do something?
- Cleaned up after yourself?
- Did your own laundry?
- Helped clean someone's house?
- Told someone you appreciate everything they do for you?
- Told someone you appreciate their friendship?
- Cooked someone a nice meal?
- Bought someone flowers?
- Bought someone a drink?
- Took someone out to dinner?
- Took someone on a small vacation?
- Took a scenic car ride?
- Took a road trip, leaving before dawn?
- Went on a scenic train ride?
- Flew somewhere exciting for a long weekend?
- Made a list of state parks in your area and visited them?
- Went for a walk?
- Took a bike ride?
- Shot darts?
- Shot pool?

- Went bowling?
- Played cards or board games with some friends?
- Went on a boat ride?
- Went to a large body of water and just hung around?
- Rented a go-cart, pontoon boat, rowboat/kayak/canoe?
- Bought some Bitcoin?
- Listened to the band Earth, Wind and Fire "That's the Way of the World?"
- Took a week off work and just lived day-to-day, doing sporadic, fun things?

Seriously, when was the last time you did anything fun? What about going to the movies? Taking a nap? When was the last time you went to a bookstore and just sat around to read? Can you remember the last time you visited a museum, aquarium, zoo, botanical garden, or even the beach? When was the last time you went to the gym? When was the last time you volunteered for some cause? When last did you tell someone, "I love you?"

You see, there are so many fun and beautiful things to do in life, but sometimes we get stuck with the many worries of life and miss out on the fun things.

Remember these pieces of advice:

- Remove yourself from confrontational situations, especially on the road.
- Choose what you think about.
- Next time you are at the whatever store, park further away on purpose to get more exercise.
- Take a walk, just to take a walk.

- Embrace change or die.
- Keep on growing.
- Right now, contact the people you love and tell them you love them.
- Learn how to cook; start with some easy stuff.
- Everything is negotiable. Learn to negotiate.

As we wrap up this book, I need you to know that you are capable of changing to be the best version of you. All it takes is a little consistent work. Create new habits; miracles happen all the time. The sun will rise tomorrow, and with it will come a better day. Learn to forgive everyone who hurts you and give your mind peace. If you offended someone, call them and apologize. Take a good look at how you are spending most of your time on this earth and understand why you are doing so.

Get closer to nature—this is way more important than you think. It's soothing. Stand around and look at the ocean or lake or any other water body close to you. Just bask in the soothing beauty of nature, and unwind. Plant something in a pot, drink more water, laugh more, and dance—it's good for you. Laugh at yourself...you're funny!

Time heals all wounds. Life will always have its ups and downs, but focus on the good, and don't be a crybaby. Collect memories rather than physical junk. The person who loves the journey will always make it further and be happier than the person who only loves the destination.

To the world, you may just be one person, but to one person, you may be the world.

You, and only you, make the rules for your own life. Always remember that you control what you think about. Think more about ideas—you might have a major breakthrough that'll help the world. As Henry Ford said, "If you think you can or think you can't, either way you're right."

Either get busy living, or get busy dying. Decide to have more fun!

Give every day of your life the chance to be the best day of your life.

The small stuff is the big stuff.

Thanks for visiting. Y'all come back soon.

You can contact me with any questions or feedback at Pat@RoadJuice.com

ABOUT THE AUTHOR

For most of us, the closest we get to delving deeply into an issue is in the few moments we can steal going from one task to another.

Patrick Cafone, a 2 million mile driver based in upstate N.Y. has spent countless hours behind the wheel windshielding creative ideas and wondering what makes life tick.

Pat is a husband, father, grandfather, gardener and musician. His passion for learning and digging deep into the fields of love, happiness, eating, driving and music has brought him to put his findings on paper to share with the world in the writing of his book "Road Juice"

www.ingramcontent.com/pod-product-compliance
Lightning Source LLC
LaVergne TN
LVHW051232080426
835513LV00016B/1549

* 9 7 9 8 8 9 3 1 6 8 8 7 7 *